AF579179

# *Pigeon Shooting*

# *Pigeon Shooting*

RICHARD ARNOLD

KAYE & WARD
LONDON

First published in Great Britain
by Faber & Faber Ltd
1956
Reprinted 1966, 1972 (with corrections)
Revised edition first published by
Kaye & Ward Ltd,
21 New Street, London EC2M 4NT
1979



ISBN 0 7182 1229 0 (*hardback*)
ISBN 0 7182 1241 X (*paperback*)
Set in Monotype Times by Gloucester Typesetting Co. Ltd.
Printed in Great Britain by Redwood Burn Ltd
Trowbridge & Esher

*To the memory of*
*that old sportsman, my grandfather,*
*Jimmy Sinclair of Edinburgh and Manchester,*
*who, in spite of strenuous parental anti-sports opposition,*
*introduced me to all field sports*
*and taught me to love the*
*creatures of the chase*

# Contents

# *Foreword*

Some 20 odd years ago I was requested by Mr Brian Vesey-Fitzgerald to write a book on 'Pigeon Shooting' for Faber & Faber Ltd.

Until that manuscript was accepted and published in 1956 no book entirely devoted to the sport of pigeon shooting had ever been published.

In my first edition I wrote about shooting matters which were completely contrary to whatever had previously been published about pigeon shooting as a sport. Until my book was published, and indeed for some little time after, sportsmen were advised to use size 4 shot: this even appeared in the ICI 'Shooter's Yearbook' as a recommendation, and was regarded by the Agricultural Executive Committees of the time as the only size to use. Today shooters have adopted my recommendation and sizes 6 and 7 are now regarded, rightly, as the best sizes to use.

Again, it was the custom to site one's decoys downwind of the shooting position: my then revolutionary suggestion to site the decoys upwind is now regarded as a matter of commonsense.

Subsequent to the first edition appearing other shooting authors produced books on pigeon shooting: I believe that apart from one still in print they have disappeared! I am very happy therefore that this new edition has been taken over by Kaye & Ward Ltd., who have earlier published several shooting and angling books of mine: principally, *The Shooter's Handbook*, *Automatic and Repeating Shotguns*, *Clay Pigeon Shooting*, and *The Book of the .22*. After almost 60 years of field shooting, this is very gratifying.

*Offord D'Arcy,*
*Huntingdon,*
*Cambridgeshire.*

RICHARD ARNOLD

CHAPTER 1

# *Introduction*

Once upon a time, when England was one huge manor, divided and sub-divided into smaller estates, when the central figure in a rural community was the Squire, shooting was confined to a select few who were both wealthy and leisured. Shooting estates were large: game preservation was carried out on a grand scale and, with the introduction of the breech-loading gun, the art of driving game was conceived. At that time, unless one was fortunate enough to have a farmer friend whose shooting rights were not let, the chances of an artisan taking up sporting shooting as a pastime were remote in the extreme. To possess a gun in those so-called halcyon days of sport was the hall-mark of the landed gentleman, the officer, or wealthy merchant. Of course, there was another side to the picture; guns were also possessed by those who sought their sport along the wrong side of the fence – the poacher, the sport-seeking individual who loved a gun for its own sake, and the professional fowler, bird-collector, and gamekeeper.

Gradually the picture changed. Shooting estates reached their highest pinnacle just before the outbreak of World War I. In those days giants, indeed, commanded the shooting field, leaving names to be conjured with to this very day. Names such as Lord Walsingham, Sir Frederick Milbank, Maharajah Duleep Singh, Rimington-Wilson, Lord Ripon, Earl de Grey, to mention but a few whose feats among sporting birds are not likely to be emulated, if indeed that were desirable, by modern sportsmen.

The Second World War (1939–45) saw a revolution in the shooting world. Many of the large manors and estates had, by force of economic circumstances between the two wars, to be sold and broken up, and when these little 'empires' of good husbandry and game-keeping were liquidated, the great shooting estates were split up into smaller estates. This led to the creation of the shooting syndicate.

A shooting syndicate has become, in some sporting circles, a cliché denoting a preying of wealthy stockbrokers and city merchants, who scarcely knowing one end of a gun from another, rented a shoot for social and business purposes, neglected the simple art of game preservation and keepering, and denuded the estate of all sporting possibilities within the period of their lease. Nothing, in actual fact, could be further from the truth. The modern shooting syndicate is purely and simply a partnership among shooting men. By clubbing together they are able to pool finances and are thereby enabled to rent a shoot, as well as retain the services of a keeper, something which individually they could not afford to undertake. The bad syndicate, the preying of stockbrokers to which I have alluded, soon finds that there is nothing worth while in continuing the shoot and therefore abandon it, and tries to find another shoot elsewhere. In such a case the shooting landlord finds that his property has decreased in value, and takes steps to ensure that in future only suitable sporting tenants become lessees. Moreover the rural grapevine generally ensures that, in due course, bad syndicates are unable to rent, retain, or purchase a shoot by any means.

The process which began the levelling down of the great estates as well as the two wars, and the industrial expansion which was involved, gave rise paradoxically to a rapid growth in the number of shooting men. Today shooting men may be counted in thousands where previously they were counted in scores. Today, with the development of the modern breech-loading gun, manufactured easily and cheaply by a machine-shop process, a vast number of sporting guns are in daily use throughout the British Isles. Unfortunately, it is true enough that modern conditions have ousted the old master craftsmen to whom time meant nothing, but to whom the finished product was everything, and true it is that the gun-trade suffers particularly in this respect. Nevertheless the machine-made shotgun is still an excellent weapon, is robustly made, and though not comparable with a hand-made gun costing up to several thousand pounds, is matched equably with its owner's income, and with care should last him most of his life.

The breaking up of the large estates was but one factor bringing shooting within the reach of the common man: the rapid growth of towns, the urbanization of the countryside, the obliteration of pastures and arable lands beneath structures of steel and concrete, brick and slate, have made a substantial proportion of our town and city dwellers country-hungry. The cult of the hiker, the passion of the bird watcher, the gatherings of Field Societies and the interest in Field Sports, are a natural consequence of this country-hunger. But, alongside this intense desire to return to the country, if only for a few precious hours, there is a realization that the natural wild life of the countryside has either been driven from its natural environments to other, more hospitable and undeveloped areas, or exterminated.

The nutbrown partridge, the pride of English game-shoots, is dwindling in numbers, so much so that there is every possibility that its close season may be extended: the men who can afford to rear, and shoot, pheasants on a princely scale are few and far between: the rabbit, once the mainstay of most artisan sportsmen, subjected to the terrible scourge of myxomatosis, almost disappeared from the shooting scene. Today it is returning, but unfortunately, whilst this country continues to import frozen rabbit at a cost of several million pounds annually from China, the British rabbit is the subject of gas and poison warfare. It no longer has the sporting place it once occupied. Grouse shooting and deer-stalking are still the prerogatives of the comparatively wealthy.

The growing number of shooters has looked with despair at the cutting back of the countryside: in that despair it has turned to the sport of wildfowling, justly acclaimed as the toughest, roughest field sport in the country. But wildfowling, through its very growth, through its increasing popularity, has attracted a great number of bad sportsmen: men who, city bred, town trained, have an urge to fire a gun at something, anything, no matter whether in season or out, lawful 'game' or protected bird. In consequence wildfowling has attracted a lot of undesirable publicity, often the fault of those writers who, in delightfully lyrical prose, have overdone the purple passages of dawn flights. The direct result of all this has been that the sport of wildfowling, thrust unwillingly into the glare of public discussion, has been made the villain of the piece so far as decrease of certain wild birds has been concerned. The Protection of Birds Act, 1954, admittedly an overdue piece of legislation, took a sizable portion of shooting away from the wildfowler.

Apart from the curtailment of its season, wildfowling cannot appeal to all shooters. The man who takes up shooting in his later years, the man who (perhaps through war injury) is unable to walk far, or who is unable to follow the sport for economic reasons must seek another outlet. Wildfowling, free to all, necessitates long travelling hours for the city sportsman who lives a considerable distance from the coast. This may well mean travelling overnight in the worst of winter's weather. To this must be added the rising costs of travel by road and the increases in the fares of public transport.

This presents a very gloomy picture to the man who, equipped by nature with a desire to shoot, surveys the possibilities of following his sport. To take part in clay-pigeon shoots may be beyond his financial means: rifle shooting on the range may bore him to tears. It is then that he finds cause to bless a bird whose depredations amongst cultivated crops has led to it being dubbed by farmers and Government alike as feathered 'Public Enemy No. 1'. So much so that a price was once put on its head to the extent of 50 per cent reduction in the cost of cartridges used in its actual or attempted destruction.

I am, of course, referring to the wild pigeon – the bird which will provide the solution to our sportsman's problem, and in addition give him the finest sport on the wing which is obtainable anywhere in the world. And, to cap it all, most pigeon shooting is free, there is no close season, the bird is found almost everywhere, and, finally, it is a delight on the table!

Strangely enough, in spite of all these advantages, pigeon shooting as a sport has received but scant attention from shooting authors in the past. Most of the early works when referring to pigeon shooting, deal only with that abomination, the shooting of pigeons released from traps, the forerunner of the modern clay-bird shooting. Of many good shooting authors, only Sir Ralph Payne Gallwey devotes anything like sufficient space to this fascinating sport. But pigeon shooting, neglected in the past, as the shooting diaries of the great estates will show, has probably the greatest number of 'wing' shooters in the country. Certainly it is the mainstay of the average rough shooter and it is certain to grow in popularity. Indeed, though only a few seasons ago the farmers were calling for the assistance of shooters to help keep down the invading hordes of pigeon, today the number of pigeon shooters is growing so quickly that farmers, who once invited shooters to destroy or drive away pigeons on their lands, faced with a decline in game shooting owing to the decrease in the partridge, and the absence of rabbits, are now asking for rentals for pigeon shooting!

Pigeon shooting may be enjoyed almost everywhere and anywhere. The birds are ubiquitous and frequent town park or garden as readily as open farmland. Even the smallest allotment will generally provide a keen sportsman with a certain amount of sport. Nor is this shooting confined to the artisan alone. Pigeon shooting is enjoyed by all classes. Pigeon shooting now forms a portion of the season's programme, even for the man who is able to shoot over the best of preserves.

'There is no kind of sport which tries more severely the nerve and skill of those who delight to handle the shotgun,' this was the opinion of wood-pigeon held by the famed Lord Walsingham himself, a sportsman without equal in the use of the shotgun, who on 27th August 1872 killed 842 grouse on the Blubberhouse Moors, and driven grouse are reputedly the most difficult of all game birds.

Even Royalty have enthused over the delights of pigeon shooting and it will be recalled that the late King George VI, an excellent shot, on the day before his sudden death in February 1952 had been out pigeon shooting on his estate at Sandringham. His last shot of the day, indeed, tragically, the last shot of his life, was at an incredibly high pigeon and the newspapers reported his keen delight and pardonable pride in pulling down this bird. No longer do the national press merely report Royalty stalking the stag, or pheasant shooting: the fact that H.R.H. The Duke of Edinburgh goes pigeon shooting alone is commented on as a news story.

It is only in England, however, that pigeon shooting has been neglected until lately. In Scotland pigeon shooting has always been a very important factor in the large shooting estates and this form of shooting, including the use of tree-top hides, has been specially catered for. South of the Tweed, however, apart from odd days organized for the agricultural workers, and odd forays after birds, the sportsmen who have appreciated the qualities of the pigeon have been small in number. Time was when the pigeon figured in the game diary with vermin, moorhens, rooks, etc., under the heading of 'various' in the game bag: nowadays it has a whole column to itself, sometimes a whole diary!

There was a reason, however, for this great neglect of the pigeon by earlier shooters. The pigeon is an unpredictable bird. It may be an easy shot one moment, and an impossible target the next. Excellent performers though some of the more famous names were, they were nevertheless in the position that they knew exactly where their birds would come from, whether grouse, partridge or pheasant: they had the knowledge of the course the birds would take, their approximate height, their speed. In other words, they were familiar with the peculiarities of their quarry which would remain constant under given conditions. But the pigeon would fool them. It was not worth while pursuing an elusive and difficult bird when much money had been spent in rearing or preserving certain game birds, so the more expensive, and comparatively easier, game birds predominated.

What are the attractions of pigeon shooting?

Perhaps the shooting poet who wrote more than 120 years ago can give us a clue:

*There's no rural sport surpasses*
*Pigeon shooting – circling glasses –*
*Fill the crystal goblet up:*
*No game laws can ever thwart us,*
*Nor* qui tams*; no habeas corpus*
*For our licence Venus grants.*
*Let's be grateful – here's a bumper;*
*For her bounty – here's a bumper;*
*'Listed under beauty's banners,*
*What's to us freehold or manors?*
*Fill the crystal goblet up.*

The attractions, summed up in modern prose, are that pigeon are not subject to the game laws: they do not need a game licence: there is no close season for them: nor is it necessary to have a large shooting estate over which to seek them. Indeed, from the ordinary shooter's point of view, and here I mean the man with little financial resources, the wood-pigeon and stock-dove are the finest sporting proposition of all.

Many legends have grown up around the pigeons themselves: that they are tough birds, capable of carrying an enormous amount of shot: that they must be shot from behind because their feathers act as armour when shot at from the front: that they demand fully choked, heavily loaded guns with large shot. All these beliefs are false and stupid, passed on from one armchair sportsman to another, accepted without enquiry.

Pigeon can be shot with an ordinary game gun, using game loads, with the smaller sizes of shot. There is no need to go to the expense of a special gun or more expensive cartridges. The pigeon's main defences are wonderful eyesight and ability to change course in a split second: it is neither armour-plated nor capable of carrying a lot of heavy shot.

1. The pigeon shooter's outfit consisting of hide mesh, camouflage clothing, monocular, decoy pigeon, ammunition, and gun.

There are five species of pigeon on the British List. Three are resident breeding birds, one a summer visitor, and one a rare vagrant. The species in order of importance are the wood-pigeon, the stock-dove, the rock-dove, the turtle-dove, and the collared-dove. This last, though at present very rare, may well at some future date, if the views of the late celebrated ornithologist, James Fisher, are correct, become a resident breeding bird in Britain.

The wood-pigeon (also known as the ring-dove, the cushat or the quist) will be the species most often encountered by the gunner, though the stock-dove (often erroneously called a 'blue rock' by sportsmen and countrymen who should know better) runs it a good second. The rock-dove is pursued by comparatively few sportsmen as its habitat is amongst the caves and crevices of the coastal cliffs. Rock-dove shooting is in itself a highly specialized form of sport and forms the subject of a later chapter.

Between the ring-dove or wood-pigeon and the stock-dove little distinction can be drawn so far as the damage they do to crops is concerned. Because of its larger numbers, the wood-pigeon is the greater enemy taking the country as a whole, but in some districts the stock-doves outnumber the wood-pigeon. In this connection it is interesting to note the mentality of certain protectionists who must protect anything and everything for the mere sake of protection! I was once taken to task by an ardent protectionist, a lady, who remonstrated with me for killing birds and rabbits 'for sport', and who concluded with the remark – 'We can exist without killing animals, birds, or fishes: I am a vegetarian.' I looked at her steadily, then down to her feet. She followed my gaze, then blushed as she understood the import of my look.

'Madam,' I said, 'I respect your views, but I'd respect your sincerity more if you didn't wear *leather* shoes.' I continued the attack – 'I have to point out to you that if I, along with others, did not kill the rabbits, and the pigeons, which eat the corn, the wheat, and the green things from which you make your vegetarian meals, you would go on short commons. In other words, madam, I kill animals so that you may eat vegetables.'

A typical example of protection gone mad was the order made in the County of Kent under the Wild Birds Protection Act – this protected the stock-dove. I should imagine, from what I saw and heard, that more shooters risked penalties in that county under that provision than any other lawbreakers elsewhere. Sufficient to state that under the Protection of Birds Act, 1954, both wood-pigeon and stock-dove are included in a special list of birds which may be killed or taken at any time by authorized persons. The legal position with regard to pigeons shooting is that under the provisions of the Protection of Birds Act, 1954, the stock-dove and the wood-pigeon receive absolutely no protection at all; the rock-dove is added to this list of 'harmful birds' in so far as Scotland is concerned. The turtle-dove and the collared-dove are protected at all times. However, though no one would wantonly shoot either of the two latter species, it may well be that farmers or gardeners may be plagued by the turtle-dove or the rock-dove in England. If he shoots one of these birds and is prosecuted for so doing, the farmer may plead a statutory defence that the shooting was necessary to prevent serious damage to crops, vegetables, growing timber or any other form of property or to fisheries (Section 4, sub-section 2 (a) of the Act) but the onus is upon him to satisfy the court that his action was justified. The sudden descent of a flock of turtle-doves or rock-doves on to a field of peas might be such an occasion. So far as the sporting gunner is concerned it is wise to steer well clear of any possibility of law-breaking and to confine shooting to those two species which he may shoot without legal restriction and which will provide him with ample sport without recourse to the less harmful and rarer birds.

There is no need to hold a game licence for pigeon shooting though under the provisions of Part V of the Criminal Justice Act 1968 a shotgun certificate, issued by your local police, is necessary. If you are a visitor to Britain, and your stay is going to be less than thirty days in a year, it will not be necessary for you to apply for a shotgun certificate. One does not need a shotgun certificate if borrowing a shotgun from the occupier of private premises, which includes private land, providing it is used in his presence.

Before venturing out on his first shooting foray after the pigeon, it is as well for the sportsman to acquaint himself thoroughly with the natural history and characteristics of the quarry. During the last war a very important part of military training consisted of learning everything of importance about the foe, his uniform, his equipment, military organizations, national characteristics, even smatterings of his language. 'Know your enemy!' was the title given to this training. 'Know your bird,' is equally important to the sporting shooter.

### *Metrication*

Unfortunately, with the introduction of metrication and the gradual elimination of our imperial system, there are now two classes in the country, the older members of the community who *think* in the old measurements and the young members who only know the metric system.

To avoid confusion, therefore, when quoting authorities before metrication, their terminology will be unchanged: but in all other cases to help over the transitional period, and also be of some assistance to my friends on the other side of the Atlantic the old terms will be used with metric equivalents immediately following, e.g. $1\frac{1}{16}$ oz. (30·1 g).

I also append below two tables. The first showing conversion of yards to metres the second showing shot charge weights in ounces, grains, and metric grammes.

*Range in yards converted to metres*

| Yards (English) | Metres | Yards (English) | Metres |
|---|---|---|---|
| 1 | 0·91 | 25 | 22·86 |
| 10 | 9·14 | 30 | 27·43 |
| 15 | 13·72 | 35 | 32·00 |
| 20 | 18·29 | 40 | 36·58 |

*Shot charge weights*

| Ounces | Grains | Grammes (Metric) |
|---|---|---|
| $\frac{1}{16}$ | 27·3 | 1·8 |
| $\frac{1}{8}$ | 54·7 | 3·5 |
| $\frac{1}{4}$ | 109·3 | 7·1 |
| $\frac{1}{2}$ | 218·7 | 14·2 |
| $\frac{3}{4}$ | 328·1 | 21·2 |
| 1 | 437·5 | 28·3 |
| $1\frac{1}{16}$ | 464·8 | 30·1 |
| $1\frac{1}{8}$ | 492·2 | 31·9 |
| $1\frac{1}{4}$ | 546·8 | 35·4 |

It is also necessary to include two other conversion tables – one for dealing with weight (principally of guns) and the other in respect of gun chamber lengths.

*Conversion of pounds (lb) to kilogrammes (kg)*

| Pounds (lb) | Kg | Pounds (lb) | Kg |
|---|---|---|---|
| 1 | 0·45 | 6 | 2·72 |
| 2 | 0·91 | 7 | 3·18 |
| 3 | 1·36 | 8 | 3·63 |
| 4 | 1·81 | 9 | 4·08 |
| 5 | 2·27 | 10 | 4·54 |

*Cartridge (and gun chamber) lengths*

| Inches | Millimetres |
|---|---|
| 2 | 50.8 |
| 2½ | 65 |
| 2¾ | 70 |
| 3 | 75 |

CHAPTER 2

# *Know Your Bird*

The wood-pigeon is more correctly termed the ring-dove as though it nests in woods, for preference, it is really a bird of the open countryside. Even here the name ring-dove is not truly descriptive because the white markings on the neck of the bird from which it gets its name are not rings at all! The white marks are on only part of the neck where the bordering feathers are darkest, thereby enhancing the contrast.

The wood-pigeon is the biggest of our British doves and is easily recognized by its grey plumage with pink-tinged breast, white neck marks, barred tail, and, when in flight, very conspicuous white wing bars. It is a most prolific breeder. Though the greatest percentage of nesting activity takes place from the end of May to the second half of July, nesting takes place from March to the end of October in a fairly regular rhythm. I have often heard shooters remark, in amazement, 'Why, that bird's doing his mating display!' when, in late September, a cock bird has appeared over the trees on the shoot, performing his thrilling gliding and soaring aerobatics. Invariably the information that pigeons breed as late as October is received with disbelief. There are, as investigators have shown, annual variations in the breeding season and the peak may be reached as early as April or as late as August. Breeding has, however, been recorded in every month of the year.

Two eggs form the normal clutch, and there is very little variation. These conspicuous white eggs are laid a day apart and incubation commences with the first one. Hatching takes place at from eighteen to twenty-one days, according, of course, to meteorological conditions – an early clutch in very cold weather probably taking a full twenty-one days through cooling of the eggs, while a midsummer clutch may take three days less. Both cock and hen bird take turns in sitting. Each pair of pigeon lays, on an average, three clutches per season, but the wood-pigeon suffers from a very heavy juvenile mortality. The sparrow-hawk, the magpie, the grey squirrel, and the rooks, take their toll and it has been assumed by some authorities that on average each pair of wood-pigeons produces $1\frac{1}{2}$ fledglings per year. Juvenile mortality after fledgling cannot be assessed accurately but a heavy mortality is fairly certain.

A characteristic of pigeons is their method of feeding their young. The young birds feed on a fatty glandular product given off from the crops of both parent birds. The chick inserts its beak into the parent's mouth and feeds on this glandular substance, known popularly as 'pigeon's milk'. After about ten days the chick is weaned gradually to grain which has been softened in the crop of the parent bird, and which it receives by a violent pumping action. Fledging normally takes about five weeks, though if the nest is subject to disturbance the young bird may leave a week or ten days earlier.

The newly hatched chick has a yellowish or creamy coloured coat of down. When about seven days old the youngster starts to grow its primaries and this growth of plumage is maintained at an even rate for about five weeks. The bill is purple-grey with a horn-coloured tip at hatching. After about five weeks the rear portion of the bill assumes a mauve hue, and after ten weeks or so the fore part of the bill, i.e. in front of the nostril, becomes yellowish, the typical adult characteristic. Whilst a juvenile the bird has brown-tipped feathers, in fact the whole wing may appear brown, and the bird is considered an adult when the last of the brownish feathers have been shed.

The nest of the wood-pigeon is merely a rough platform of sticks, and it is surprising how this apparently frail structure will often survive winter gales. Although preferring to breed in the woodlands, the wood-pigeon will nest in gardens, and in the Orkneys they build their nests on the ground, constructing them of twigs and grass.

The largest percentage of nests will be found in evergreen trees and shrubs during early spring and autumn. Summer breeding pairs show their greatest percentage of nests amongst deciduous trees, preferably those covered with ivy, since these provide the maximum cover. Of the evergreen trees and shrubs favoured at the beginning and end of the breeding period, conifers are the most favoured. Hedgerows containing hawthorn bushes, elder bushes, are sites with ideal nesting situations, and if the cover is very thick the pigeons will prefer to nest in these surroundings rather than in trees. But pigeons utilize high trees as look-out posts, and a shrubbery or hedgerow without such a point will not contain many wood-pigeon nests.

There is no favourite height at which these birds erect their nests. In view of their wary and nervous disposition one would imagine that their nests would be placed fairly high. In actual fact, in parks, cemeteries, and gardens where mankind and cats are likely to be disturbing factors, the wood-pigeon does place its nest higher than in the woods. Nests have a marked tendency to be placed lower in fields and moorland country than in woodland country. In general nests are placed higher at the beginning and end of the breeding period. From ten feet to fifteen feet (3–4·5 m) may be taken as a fairly average height throughout the year. Wood-pigeons are gregarious birds and gather together in large flocks during the winter. Unlike other gregarious birds (such as the rook) they do not nest in 'colonies', the nests being distributed fairly evenly throughout the breeding habitat.

A peculiar fact about breeding pigeon is that, although there may be a high breeding density in a particular wood, there is never a great deal of evidence of this during the incubation period when the birds are sitting. It is only as the season advances, when the birds are heard, and there is unmistakable evidence in the form of shed flight and tail feathers in the undergrowth, and the presence of egg-shells on the ground, that the density of breeding is appreciated. It is essential, therefore, to enter and explore potential breeding sites regularly and thoroughly.

The breeding display flight, to which I have alluded earlier, consists of a distinctive wing-clap and swooping glide. This is most frequently seen in early spring and late summer and as a rule a displaying bird is often accompanied by a third party going through the same drill! 'Two's company' is not apparently appreciated by courting pigeons!

Of all our native birds, the wood-pigeon is probably the most harmful to agriculture. Its food consists of wheat, oats, barley, rye, beans, peas, cabbage, rape, turnip tops, swedes, potatoes, clover leaves, sprouting grain, and fruit. Additionally, wild fruits such as acorns, haws, wild berries are taken and a considerable amount of weeds, such as dock, chickweed, and charlock is consumed. The wood-pigeon is a very greedy feeder and over a thousand grains of wheat have been taken from the crop of one pigeon. Nearly 200 peas found in the crop of a bird which I shot at Barnet in 1954 (187 peas to be exact), will give an idea of the damage which this bird can inflict on crops.

The pigeon attacks the exposed grains in newly drilled fields, wheat being the favourite food, followed by barley and oats. The pigeon does not dig for its food, and does not stay long on a newly sown field. When the birds have cleared up the surface seed, they leave the cereal crops alone until the grain has formed. If, when the corn is green, birds are shot there, their crops will contain weed seeds or leaves, *not* corn. But as soon as the grain is in the 'milk', it will be subjected to attack. If corn or wheat has been flattened by wind or rain, the wood-pigeons are soon attracted to the area and the damage they will do is heartbreaking to the farmer concerned as in addition to the grain consumed, many heads of corn are fouled by the droppings.

Clover is a popular food, particularly in the seedling stage, broad red clover being the most favoured. The hearts of the clover are not taken, but seedling plants are denuded of leaves.

Freshly sown peas are a great attraction. It is not unusual for wood-pigeon to be seen feeding on peas which have been exposed by wireworm-hunting rooks. The leaves and tips of the peas are taken when the crop begins to appear above the ground, and at harvest time pigeon are very prone to attack a pea crop. Beans also suffer from the depredations of these birds but, as the seeds are often ploughed in and not drilled, they suffer less than peas. Pigeons do not eat the leaves of seedling beans.

During the winter months kale, cabbage and rape form part of the pigeon's food. In time of snow the birds will strip the brassicas to the midrib, and, of course, with their heavy droppings, may foul and rot the crowns of the plants. Generally speaking, however, greens are attacked in severe winter weather. Pigeons also attack young roots and injured roots are, of course, subject to damage and decay from frost and damp. Linseed capsules and seeds are also taken and damage by wood-pigeons to this valuable crop has been considerable in the past. Pigeons are also very fond of eating potatoes which have been left in the fields and turned up by ploughing.

The shooter should remember that pigeons which have fed on root crops, such as turnips, are not as good on the table as those which have fed on cereals and legumes. If a bird is shot and it is found that the crop is full of turnip tops, the crop should be emptied immediately, otherwise the bird will be rancid and sour in taste. In this connection

Gilbert White writing of the stock-dove, which he erroneously called 'rockiers', remarks:

'But of late years, since the vast increase of turnips, that vegetable has furnished a great part of their support in hard weather; and the holes they pick in these roots greatly damage the crop. From this food their flesh has contracted a rancidness, which occasions them to be rejected by nicer judges of eating, who thought them before a delicate dish.' (Letter XCIV, 30th November 1780—*Natural History of Selborne*.)

Again, he recounts an incident which may seem barbarous to modern tastes:

'One of my neighbours shot a ring-dove on an evening as it was returning from feed and going to roost. When his wife had picked and drawn it, she found its craw stuffed with the most nice and tender tops of turnip. These she washed and boiled, and so sat down to a choice and delicate plate of greens, culled and provided in this extraordinary manner.'

Other foods, principally during the months of May and June, are the weeds growing amongst the cereals. During this period the pigeons are feeding on corn pansy, buttercup and so on, and are not, in actual fact, attacking the corn itself. Beech-mast is a very important food and where these, as well as acorns, are freely available, the birds will prefer to feed on them rather than on cultivated crops.

In addition to the foregoing vegetable diets, I have shot pigeon which, on examination of their crops, seemed to have been feeding exclusively on small snails. Two birds whose crops I examined contained over 800 of these tiny snails, so it would appear that they were doing a certain amount by way of reparation. Earthworms have also been found in pigeon's crops. The snails were taken during the very hot summer months and this seems to fall in line with a recent theory that the pigeon take these for their moisture content as well as an alternative to grit.

Bearing in mind the times of the year when the pigeon is likely to feed on certain foods, the shooter is able to plan his campaign for successful sport.

The following table will give a rough indication of the pigeon's feeding almanac.

| *Month* | *Food* |
|---|---|
| January | Ivy berries, cultivated brassicas, weeds, clover, turnip tops, tops of greens, cabbages. |
| February | Weeds, clover, tops of green crops. |
| March | Sowings of peas and beans, clovers. |
| April | Sowings of peas, clovers, seed corn, early shoots, weeds. |
| May | Weeds (the main food): garden crops, peas, clover. |
| June | Weeds principally. |
| July | Corn, peas, weeds, snails. |
| August | Peas, corn crops. |
| September | Stubble gleaning. |
| October | Newly drilled cereals, stubble, covert food. |
| November | Wild fruits, hips, haws, acorns, beech-mast. |
| December | As in November – with weeds and tops of greens. |

The above is by no means exhaustive, and there is, of course, considerable overlapping between the months.

By way of interest, Messrs. I.C.I. Ltd., state that five sample crop contents of the wood-pigeon included respectively, 61 acorns, 28 hazel nuts, 270 beech nuts, 20 small potatoes, and 203 ivy berries. I have often shot wood-pigeons which included hazel nuts in their crops and have wondered at their powers of digestion. Part of my shooting, over 300 acres (121 ha) of wild woodland, has revealed that the seed cases of the common bluebell are a favourite food of these birds, though strange to relate, these did not impart a bitter flavour to their flesh as one would expect.

Mr. Owen Jones, who wrote under the pen-name of 'Gamekeeper' half a century ago, has stated in his entertaining and informative book *Ten Years of Gamekeeping*:

'Many a time I have supplied my fowls with a meal of grain emptied from the crops of pigeons I had shot. A keeper acquaintance one autumn was waiting for pigeons which fed on some barley stubble; and to pass away the intervals between the arrivals of the birds, he counted the grains of barley in the crop of one pigeon. There were a thousand and thirty-three, besides a few small snail-shells.'

A bag of a couple of dozen pigeon in these circumstances would give quite easily a reasonable feed to a few hens so that Mr. Jones's statement is not so wild as might at first appear to the uninitiated in the ways of wild pigeons.

It has been estimated that one wood-pigeon consumes not less than 1¾ oz. (50 g) of food per day, so that 100 birds may eat almost 1 stone (over 6 kg) of food in that period: likewise a thousand pigeon eat at least 1 cwt. (50 kg) per day! It is little wonder, therefore, that an all-out war is being waged against them by the agriculturalists. As much as 4 oz. (115 g) of haws have been found in the crop of a single bird.

The crop is a rather peculiar organ. It acts simply as a storehouse for the food, and when the crop is empty, food passes directly to the bird's gizzard. A full crop has periodical contractions of its walls which force a further supply of food into the gizzard. A continuous process of receiving and passing on food is undergone by the crop during the day. Pigeons have an empty crop in the mornings, and, in the winter in particular, have a full crop at evening.

For many years it has been 'understood' by countrymen and shooting men that in the winter months we suffer an invasion of 'foreign' wood-pigeons. Unfortunately there have been few experiments in the ringing of wood-pigeons and recoveries of those ringed have been very small. *There is no evidence, only a belief which has not been proved, that wood-pigeons migrate to or from Britain.*

It was something of a bombshell to shooting men when the Agricultural Research Council reported that 'There is a certain amount of cross-Channel traffic, as shown by records of light-vessels, lighthouses, and by ringed birds, but these represent irregular wanderings, mainly by juvenile birds, and not migration.'

The report, which caused such a furore in the shooting press, then went on to state:

'To sum up, the so-called "foreign" wood-pigeons are really juveniles. Flocks of wood-pigeons are seen in winter in East Anglia and elsewhere which seem too large for the resident breeding stock, but no proof has been offered that such birds come from abroad.'

Finally, the report concluded that the birds mistaken for 'foreigners' are migrants from Scotland. During its investigations in winter population of the wood-pigeon in Norfolk, the Agricultural Research Council workers examined the evidence of local observers. These local observers were of the opinion that wood-pigeons were most abundant in November, others thought January saw the greatest number of arrivals. Out of twenty observers, seventeen stated that the birds arrived from abroad, i.e. were 'foreigners', but of these seventeen, six had no evidence at all, nine gave descriptions of juvenile birds, and only two stated that they saw them arriving. This statement, contrasted with the opinions of a team of observers who conclude that the main migrational stream, or 'fly-way' to borrow a very descriptive Americanism, runs east of the Pennines from Edinburgh to south-east England. The indentations of the eastern coastline, particularly in the region of the Wash, would mean that birds on this 'fly-way' would appear to come in from over the sea. Furthermore it should be borne in mind, and this is not stressed in the report, that the prevailing winds in these Islands are from a westerly direction. Birds on migration, flying on the course given would tend to be blown out over the North Sea as they would suffer from the effects of drift. To come in to their destination they would turn into the wind and the resultant *curved* path of flight would give the impression to the casual observer that the birds did in fact come in from the Continent or Scandinavia. Add to this the admission, readily given in the report, that there is a certain amount of cross-Channel traffic and the picture held in the past that we suffered an influx of migrant pigeon from the Continent would be conjured up easily. The late T. A. Coward, widely recognized as a great authority, believed it:

'It is not proved that any of our resident ring-doves migrate, but too well known that birds in the northern part of their European and Asiatic range travel south when food supplies are precarious, for in autumn and winter great numbers arrive on the east coast . . .' and 'Though some immigrants arrive in October, the biggest hordes come in during the next three months . . . the numbers coming in from the North Sea are beyond all calculation.' (*Birds of the British Isles and Their Eggs*).

Mr. A. W. Boyd, in revised and up-to-date editions of this work states:

'Immigrants from Scandinavia begin to arrive in September, and there are often large invasions of ring-doves in November.'

The *impartial* student will request naturally on what *evidence* Mr. Coward and Mr. Boyd based their statement. It must be borne in mind that though this invasion by 'Continental' or 'foreign' wood-pigeons has been believed for many years, it is only a belief passed on from generation to generation of countrymen and there appears, on due investigation, not to be any reliable evidence at all to support it. It is safe to assume that the new theory that the invading hordes of wood-pigeon are Scottish birds, principally juveniles, is the correct answer to the problem.

When an idea is taken hold of by countrymen, and country sportsmen in particular, it is extremely difficult, if not impossible, to convince them that what they have held to be sacred truth is in fact a theory built on false premises. One can imagine how difficult it was to eradicate from the average person's mind the once popular belief that swallows hibernated for the winter in the mud in the bottom of ponds, or that barnacle geese originated from the barnacles on ships' bottoms. To modern ideas these theories seem quaint and ridiculous – no less quaint will a succeeding generation think many widely held beliefs regarding country matters in this enlightened age, not the least the theory that our winter population of wood-pigeon in England is a 'continental' invasion. Unfortunately, and the shooting man must take cognizance of this fact, there is a certain coterie of shooters who, professing a keen interest in natural history and claiming to be better ornithologists than most, automatically regard any pronouncement on the subject of wild birds, particularly birds which form the target for the gun, as erroneous in principle if it does not fit in with their preconceived ideas. The more so is this attitude pronounced if the statement emanates from the scientific researches of *conscientous and impartial* observers; yet they unhesitatingly accept earlier authorities without proof! There is, I regret to write, a tendency by some sportsmen who should know better to regard bird watching as a cult, pursued by cranks who are opposed to the man with the gun. Unfortunately these opinions, so often voiced in public, so often appearing in print, do tend to widen the rift between the genuine sportsman and the ornithologist, and the latter cannot be blamed if he is tempted to regard the shooter as either intolerant or ignorant where natural history is concerned.

The shooter, whether he pursues the pigeon, or any other bird, must become a good naturalist if he is to obtain the utmost enjoyment from his sport. In natural history matters he must retain an open mind because the whole structure of natural history theory has changed in the last two generations, and we are only on the very threshold of knowledge. If a man has the sole idea of going off into a wood or marsh, field or moor with the object of firing his gun and killing as many birds as possible in as short a time as he is able, he is neither sportsman nor naturalist. There may be times, especially in pigeon shooting, when it is necessary to indulge in tactics which would be regarded as 'unsporting' in other branches of the sport, but these will only arise when it is necessary to save crops, or to control, immediately, an influx of vermin. Though perhaps many birds will be slain in the process, the true sportsman will have no joy in the process. The measures I have in mind are browning flocks, shooting nests out of trees with either the parent birds, or parents and eggs, or young in them. The process is then one of execution and certainly does not give one a feeling of exhilaration.

What the population of wood-pigeon is in the British Isles cannot even be imagined. It must be immense because though enormous bags of them have been made, especially in the past few years under shoots organized by the various county pest officers, their numbers seem undiminished. Certainly, had any other wild bird on the sporting list, for example the widgeon or the partridge, been slain in similar numbers a very substantial step would have been taken towards their extinction. Consider but one instance: in 1954, the top 'registered' gun for the Bedfordshire Agricultural Committee, shot 3,600 pigeons between March and October! A detailed report of every shot bird was made, and wounded or 'lost' birds were excluded. Not every pigeon shooter can hope, in the nature of things, to even approach this 'record', but there must be many hundreds of sportsmen in the country today who can claim 500 pigeon or more per season. Certainly there are several score who can claim the 1,000.

Wood-pigeon populations vary from year to year. Changing agricultural methods, even metreorological conditions can disperse birds from one area, or bring about an influx of their numbers. For example, autumn sport is increased by drilling of winter cereals, but is followed by a proportionate decrease the following spring. When spring cereals are the main feature of an arable farm there is good sport when these are drilled but fewer pigeon on the fields in the autumn. During the mid-70s the sporting papers were full of queries – 'Where have the woodies gone?' It was assumed that they were being decimated, chiefly because high prices were paid for them by freezer companies and exporters of foods. Certainly there was a good market for British wood-pigeons in Italy, for example. There was also no doubt but that shooters (I would not call them sportsmen) were obsessed with the idea of shooting for gain only. Typical of letters to the shooting press was one from an RAF officer at Brampton, in Huntingdonshire. He was wont to press for a close season for woodies! Now I shoot several times a week over farms and agricultural land all around Brampton and within three miles (4·8 km) of it. I encountered no lack of pigeons and had good sport. But unless one is a regular visitor to a farm or shoot it is easy to miss pigeons on the feed because of a fold in the ground: high crops, and so on.

2. Wood pigeon. Note the characteristic white neck patches.

In East Anglia the fields are very large and pigeons can fly in at a great height and drop on to feed without one being able to contact them. Furthermore increased shooting made birds wilder, so that they quickly departed to less dangerous fields. The drought of 1975 was, no doubt, responsible for a decrease in pigeons, particularly amongst young birds. And the pigeon is catholic in its choice of foods, so that when shooters found no birds on their usual haunts they did not cast about for alternate feeds: pigeon leaving the fields could be found in the woods, enjoying the beech-mast and like.

3. Stock-dove.

The war on the grey squirrel no doubt helped the numbers of pigeons to increase, as the pigeon nests, containing eggs and young birds, are a good source of food for the squirrel. But, with grey squirrels again on the increase inevitably they are making inroads into the pigeon population.

However, today, with high costs of cartridges, and high costs of transport, there are no longer the same number of cash-conscious bounty hunting cowboy shooters about – there are plenty of pigeons for good shooting, and certainly this winter (1977) good, large flocks on a scale comparable with half-a-decade earlier are to be seen.

I would not wish to see the pigeon exterminated – nor would any of my farmer friends – but I maintain that the hysterical shouting by shooters of 1973–1975 demanding a close season for wood-pigeon was founded on lack of experience, lack of country craft, and a veritable 'do-gooder' exercise. It was noticeable that these protesters had their letters published in the shooting papers – but not in the agricultural press!

Changing cropping methods can alter the density of local pigeon populations. Today stubble is burnt off or turned in almost immediately and pigeon shooting over stubble practically a thing of the past. But, with the increase of rape acreage, pigeon shooting in areas where rape is grown is on the increase. How accurate the figures are and how they are estimated is an unresolved question but in 1977 WAGBI estimated a British wood-pigeon population of 8–10,000,000. If the calculations were based on observations by the sort of sportsman complaining about a scarcity of pigeon, a lot must have gone uncounted, because in 1976, for example, an almost record acorn and beech-mast year, shooters were complaining that the wood-pigeons were few in numbers on the fields. They were right; the birds were feeding in the woods.

Such then is the wood-pigeon, the ring-dove, the greatest feathered menace to agriculture today; yet the bird who is one of the grandest sporting birds of the British List: the bird who has been named as the British Widlfowl of the waterless districts, and of whom one gamekeeper-author has claimed: 'The man who can hit wood-pigeons can hit anything that flies.'

The stock-dove is a smaller bird. It is very common throughout many parts of the country and its feeding habits are the same. Its numbers are apt to fluctuate from year to year and in some seasons it even outnumbers the wood-pigeon.

Though apparently faster on the wing than its larger relative, it has not got the cunning eye and nervous disposition of the wood-pigeon and is easier to come to terms with. Often it is termed the 'blue rock' or 'rockier', but this is extremely misleading. The name 'stock' has been attributed to the belief that the domestic pigeon is descended from it: but this again is false, the domestic bird being a descendant of the genuine rock-dove. One other, and more reasonable interpretation of the name is that it originated from the bird's habit of building its flimsy, careless structure of a nest in the 'stock' of a hollow tree. Occasionally the bird will nest in a hole in a cliff or ruin, and nests have been recorded in rabbit burrows. The eggs, like those of the wood-pigeon, are two in number, and white in colour. Usually a male and female chick are hatched and this has given rise to the Scottish saying describing a family of one son and daughter – 'a doo's nest'.

The stock-dove prefers to travel in small flocks rather than in odd couples or single birds and these often swing round a shooter after having been fired at, giving him a further opportunity, a thing which hardly ever happens in the case of the wood-pigeon.

Feeding habits are very similar to that of the wood-pigeon and the time-table set out for that bird applies equally as well to the species under discussion.

The stock-dove is blue-grey in colour, but lacking the conspicuous white collar patches and white rump of the wood-pigeon, and there are no white bands on the wings. The neck has a much more pronounced metallic green sheen than the neck of the 'woodie'.

Though the wood-pigeon is found in many thousands in Scotland, the stock-dove is seldom found far northward, preferring the warmer districts.

The rock-dove, or 'blue rock', has received its name from its habit of frequenting rocks and cliffs, preferably on the coast. It is a common bird in Scotland, and also on the east coast of Britain, principally in Yorkshire. The domestic pigeon is undoubtedly a descendant of this bird, and when they go 'wild' they take to rocks or buildings in order to nest and rarely trouble to resort to trees. The species is very widely distributed throughout Europe and North Africa.

The rock-dove is the smallest of the British pigeons on the shooting list, and is distinguished from the stock-dove by the black bands on the wings and conspicuous white rump. As with its cousins, the eggs are white in colour and two in number. Feeding habits are similar but because of their smaller numbers nothing like the amount of damage is caused to agriculture, though the sudden descent of a flock of rock-doves on to a croft may well be disastrous for the crofter concerned. One peculiarity of this species is its ability to drink salt water.

I have come across many colonies of rock-doves in England, principally in the Pennines in Yorkshire and also in the Rossendale Valley in industrial Lancashire. They inhabit the steep cliffs as well as the old quarry workings and disused 'delphs'. There can be little doubt but that these particular colonies consist of domestic birds which have reverted to the wild state and, through successive generations of breedings, produced a true rock-dove. They give the trickiest of shots, completely unlike their larger cousins, and this branch of pigeon shooting is a highly specialized pastime.

In addition to the foregoing notes on wild pigeons, the following descriptions of the species may assist the sportsman in identification and be of some value in the construction of decoys.

*Wood-pigeon, ring-dove, Cushat* (*Columba palumbus*)

*Colour.* Head, chin, part of neck – blue-grey.
Remainder of neck, the breast – purple-red.
Distinctive white patch on neck.
Patch of skin at the base of the beak – greyish-white.
Upper parts of the body – slatey blue-grey.
Wings – slatey blue-grey with black shafts to primary quill feathers, a narrow white strip extending along the edges of the outer webs.
Wing-coverts – blue-grey with patching of whitish feathers. White patch displayed when wing open.
Tail – several varying shades of grey to black.
Under-side – white pearly grey.
*Length.* About seventeen inches (430 mm).

*Stock-dove* ('blue rock') (*Columba oenas*)

*Colour.* Head, neck, back, wing-coverts – bluish-grey.
Primary quill feathers – darker blue-grey.
Secondaries – pearl-grey with deeper coloured tips.
Tertials – blue-grey.
Chin – blue-grey: with sides of neck – slatey-grey with green gloss.
Breast – purplish.
The bird receives its scientific name *oenas* from the 'wine-coloured' tint of the throat.

The whole of the under parts are grey. The outside feathers of the vari-toned grey tail have the basal portion of the outer web white.

Beak – deep orange.

Legs – red.

*Length.* About fourteen inches (355 mm).

*Rock-dove* (*Columba livia*)

*Colour.* Head – grey. Neck – grey shot with purple and green. Chin – blue-grey. Throat – greenish-purple lustre.

Upper surface of body – grey.

Wing-primaries – grey barred with black at the tip – imparting a black band to the wing.

Second black band made by black-tipped tertials.

Lower part of the back – pure white.

Upper tail-coverts, breast, abdomen – pearl-grey.

*Length.* About twelve inches (305 mm).

CHAPTER 3

# *The Gun and Cartridge*

---

Throughout sporting literature the pigeon is described as the toughest bird that flies, able to carry a large amount of shot. And, in view of this, it is natural that large shot, magnum or long-chambered guns and heavy loads are advised as necessary. It is also natural that the average shooter, who has probably tried, with perhaps little success, to come to terms with these birds, will despair a little. His despair may well be imagined if pigeon shooting is the only form of sport he has any chance of indulging in and his armament is, according to the type of 'authority' quoted, inadequate. Add to this the fact that his finances may be such that the purchase of another gun may be completely out of the question and one more enthusiast may have been lost; unnecessarily as it happens.

Take, for instance, the appellation 'pigeon gun' which is given to $2\frac{3}{4}$-inch (70 mm) chambered 12-bores. The immediate effect of this description is to place pigeon in the same category as wildfowl, so far as the average reader is concerned. In actual fact the average game gun, i.e. *the normal $2\frac{1}{2}$-inch* (*65 mm*) *chambered 12-bore gun, using standard game load cartridges, is sufficient for pigeon shooting.*

Many shooters have, in the past, come to me for advice about the sufficiency of their particular gun for shooting wood-pigeon and wildfowl. They have, invariably, been a little distressed because the only gun they possess is a normal game gun, perhaps bored improved cylinder in the right barrel and a little choke in the left. The shooting literature they have read, the various letters in the correspondence columns of sporting papers, have raised grave doubts in their minds as to the advisability of using their apparently underpowered weapons. Because they cannot afford to purchase a new gun, perhaps also because they do not wish to part with their treasured 'friend' in exchange for a more powerful, and heavier, gun, they imagine that they will be unable to come to terms with these so-called tough, armour-plated, winged targets.

It cannot be too strongly emphasized that the term 'pigeon gun' does *not* refer to the sport of shooting wild pigeons. This term is a hang-over from the barbarous days, not so long ago, when pigeons were released from traps to form living targets for the marksmanship of 'sportsmen' whose main, indeed probably sole, interest was in the heavy wagering which accompanied this pastime, for it cannot be called a 'sport'.

That recreation, which commenced in the days of the old muzzle-loaders, resulted in competitors using larger and heavier loads in order to gain an advantage over their opponents. The advent of the breech-loader saw the introduction of slightly smaller loads in the standard 12-bore. The standard charge for a muzzle-loading 12-bore was $1\frac{1}{4}$ oz. (35·4 g) of shot with three drams of black powder. The breech-loader standard charge became $1\frac{1}{8}$ oz. (31·9 g) of shot with a similar powder charge. To allow the sportsman to shoot $1\frac{1}{4}$ oz. (35·4 g) of shot without decreasing the powder load it became necessary to employ longer cartridges, which, in turn, necessitated a longer chamber. The result was the introduction of the $2\frac{3}{4}$-inch (70 mm) chambered gun. Wildfowlers in turn developed the magnum 12-bore, utilizing longer cartridges with heavier loads and having a 3-inch (75 mm) chamber, i.e. $\frac{1}{2}$-inch (13 mm) longer than standard.

If, therefore, when perusing catalogues and price lists issued by various gunmakers, the sportsman will ignore the description 'pigeon gun' and adopt a more truly correct term, perhaps borrowing an example from the wine-merchants and calling it a 'half-magnum', he will automatically reject the necessity for a heavy gun in pigeon shooting.

Let it be stated here (and this is of the utmost importance to the sportsman no matter what his quarry is), that the first and foremost essential is to use your field-craft and woodcraft to get as near as possible to the wild creature you are seeking. If the pigeon shooter goes about his job properly (and in the following pages I hope to be able to assist him to do so) he should never need long-range weapons. There may be circumstances in wildfowling when a very powerful gun is required. In pigeon shooting the use of heavy shot leads and magnum is a confession of failure on the part of the shooter, an admission that his woodcraft is inadequate and that he relies upon long shots, which invariably result in many wounded and lost birds, to accomplish his ends.

The choice of weapon depends upon the stature, age, and physical condition of the sportsman as well as upon the extent of his purse. It is useless for an ageing man, or a slightly built youngster, or a lady, to acquire a heavy gun for pigeon shooting if the extra weight and extra recoil are uncomfortable. It must be remembered also that balance being equal, a lighter gun is more easily aimed and swung than a heavier one, particularly at the end of a long day. I have known sportsmen fail miserably with a powerful gun, simply because they were physically unable to handle the heavy weapon properly. This alone is a very strong argument against the use of heavy guns for pigeon shooting. Furthermore pigeon shooting often has moments when the shooter has to be quick, very quick, and the extra few ounces in weight may spell failure.

Personally, I recommend my own practice for successful pigeon shooting. A light 12-bore, double-barrelled, shooting the standard case with 1 oz. (28·3 g) to $1\frac{1}{8}$ oz. (31·9 g) of shot, sizes 6 or 7, with the barrels bored improved cylinder and quarter-choke, will account for most pigeon shooting occasions as highly successful. If I have to do a lot of shooting, I prefer a heavier gun, which absorbs a considerable amount of recoil, particularly so if the day is warm and a minimum of clothing is worn. For roost shooting, or high-shooting at very high birds, three quarter to full choked barrels, with the same cartridge and shot sizes as before will prove ideal. Provided, of course, that the shooter is able to hold his gun straight and judges the distances and speeds of the birds correctly.

For most of my shooting I use the ICI 'Super Trapshooting' cartridges with $1\frac{1}{8}$ oz. (31·9 g) of 7's. They give an excellent pattern and are very consistent: furthermore they can be used on most game, including pheasants.

With regard to the sportsman's purse – this is his own personal problem. Let it be said that if he is already in possession of a gun which suits him, with which he is familiar and, above all, in which he has confidence, let him retain it for use against the pigeons. It matters not whether it is an old hammer gun or a modern hammerless ejector, whether it is a 10-bore fowling piece, or a light 16-bore: if the above requirements are satisfied, then that gun will be adequte. However, if he is purchasing a gun, let it be the very best that his pocket can afford, or that his bank manager will allow him. Do not stint the price of your gun, it will have to last you many seasons, perhaps all of your life, and though the initial outlay may seem heavy, with care in selection, with diligence in maintenance and cleaning, that initial outlay becomes very little when spread over a period of, say, ten or twenty or more years. Many gunsmiths nowadays sell their guns on hire purchase terms. I cannot advice on this question because, excellent system though it is in many ways, it has been abused in the past and will no doubt continue to be abused in the future. However, if the sportsman looks at the matter steadily, does not let himself get carried away by the sight and feel of a first-class weapon and thereby enter into financial obligations which may well become a burden to him, there is a lot to be said for this method of acquiring a gun.

This subject cropped up in conversation with a well-known London gunsmith one day. His opinion is well worth recording.

'Suppose,' he said, 'a man wishes to purchase a double gun. Non-ejector for reasons of economy. Suppose that though there are many single-barrel guns on the market at a price he can easily afford the double is beyond his immediate means. There is no earthly reason why he cannot lay out the cash he has saved for the single on a good double and pay the balance by payments suited to his pocket.'

He went on further. 'One can buy a nice double non-ejector, second-hand. Remember, however, that the gun has probably had twenty years' hard wear out of it. Though we can, and do, overhaul them, do them up, re-proof them, and alter them to suit a customer's requirements, the fact remains that twenty years of that gun's life have gone. On the other hand a new gun is a *new* gun and you start off with that twenty years in hand.'

Furthermore, as he explained, the purchaser by this system has the use of his gun immediately and is using it while paying for it. If he had to save up for the initial heavy outlay required, though he would obtain the weapon ultimately, he would lose at least one whole season's shooting and a season lost can never be regained.

The prices of guns and the choice put before the shooter are bewildering in their variety, but certain facts should be borne in mind before contemplating any purchase at all, on whatever terms.

1. Never purchase a gun that has not been nitro-proved.
2. Do not purchase any gun which shows any sign of neglect in maintenance, e.g. rusty trigger guard, damaged stock, dented barrels, pitted barrels.
3. Avoid all guns which are described in advertisements as 'hard hitters', 'sure killers' and so forth. The only 'hard hitting' they

will do is in the form of recoil inflicted on the unfortunate shooter: the only 'sure killing' is the likelihood of a burst barrel or breech which removes the sportsman from this world.

It is far better for the sportsman to go along to a reputable gunsmith, and the best safeguard he has in this respect is to make sure that the gunsmith he visits is a member of the Gunmakers' Association Ltd. He should tell the gunsmith the amount he can pay and the use for which he requires the weapon – he will not suffer if he is frank.

If the sportsman is already in possession of an old black-powder gun, that is a gun which is unproved for modern nitro-powders, then he should either have the gun reproved or use only black-powder cartridges. Under no circumstances should he use modern nitro-powders in these guns as they are liable to burst under the heavier pressures generated. I know that many sportsmen, chiefly country-men, do use modern cartridges in these old guns. The fact that they have got away with it up to the moment doesn't mean a thing. Sooner or later the gun will burst, no matter whether made by Purdey or an obscure foreign gun-maker, and when a gun bursts the shooter is fortunate indeed if he incurs only minor injury. Death, blindness, permanent disfigurement, or loss of a limb are the usual consequences of this folly. I firmly believe that some day this country will see not one or two, but a whole series of accidents when these old guns begin to give up the ghost. No matter that such a gun will seem to shoot well and with safety when using modern cartridges, no matter that the gun appears sound, it must be remembered – and this cannot be emphasized too strongly – *a gun which bursts through excessive powder pressures never gives the shooter a warning beforehand.*

There is an additional safeguard in purchasing a gun from a reputable gunsmith: he will not sell a gun which has not been nitro-proved, unless, of course, he sells a black-powdered proved muzzle-loader to some muzzle-loading enthusiast.

If the sportsman who uses a black-powder gun loads his own cartridges the problem is solved for him as he may make use of black-powder for that purpose, subject of course to obtaining police permission to purchase and store this propellent. However, he will find that if he loads modern cartridge cases he will not be able to use a full black-powder charge of three drams (in a 12-bore) with a $1\frac{1}{8}$ oz. (31·9 g) of shot as the present cartridge cases, using condensed powders, have a cone in their base.

Assuming that the sportsman is about to purchase a new gun, the following points should be considered.

An average 12-bore game gun, $2\frac{1}{2}$-inch (65 mm) chambers, should weigh not less than $6\frac{1}{4}$ lb. (2·83 kg). About $6\frac{1}{2}$ lb. (2·94 kg) is a suitable weight.

An average $2\frac{3}{4}$-inch (70 mm) – 'half-magnum' gun – should weigh not less than 7 lb. – $7\frac{1}{4}$ lb. (3·30 kg) is a nice weight, though some guns may run more.

A full 'magnum' or wildfowl 12-bore, bored for 3-inch (75 mm) chambers, will certainly weigh in the region of 8 lb. (3·63 kg.)

Thus it will be seen that there is a considerable difference in the weights of guns alone: take also into consideration the fact that the longer cartridges, carrying a heavier shot load, weigh more per box of twenty-five rounds, and it will be seen how great a disadvantage the less powerful shooter is at by using a big gun.

Both double and single guns should weigh approximately the same.

There are many good single-barrelled guns on the market, and at prices well below the cost of a double gun these are probably the most suitable types of gun for the average sportsman who wishes to go pigeon shooting.

There are some points which the sportsman may wish to browse over when comparing a double gun with a single. Most shooters find that a single-barrel, with its narrower tube and sighting plane, is easier to align on the target, and that when using singles their skill improves. Against that, however, must be set the advantage that a double has over a single:

(*a*) In the event of an obstruction in the barrel which cannot be removed on the spot, the single barrel is put out of action, perhaps for the rest of the day's sport, whereas the double can carry on in such circumstances as a single.

(*b*) Any double can be used as a single if the sportsman so wishes.

(*c*) A double does enable the sportsman to take two shots; gives him the chance to shoot two different birds.

(*d*) In the event of a bird being winged by one shot, the double has the advantage that a second shot may be given to the bird, putting an end to its sufferings.

This latter point does not mean, of course, that chancy shots can be taken because the gunner has a double gun. On the contrary, the double gun, if bored with two different degrees of choke, allows the sportsman a degree of choice to obtain the best killing pattern from his gun. All shots at game or vermin, whether by double or repeating gun, should be undertaken as if the gun were a single loader.

To summarize, let the sportsman choose the gun best suited to his personal circumstances with preference for a double gun wherever possible, at a weight of between $6\frac{1}{4}$ to $6\frac{1}{2}$ lb. (2·83 to 2·94 kg) chambered for ordinary game cartridges.

In addition to shotguns, pigeon may be killed by the skilful use of the miniature rifle (·22 calibre) and the more powerful type of air rifles.

If the sportsman uses a ·22 rifle, he should make sure that his Firearms Certificate allows him to indulge in sporting shooting. Some certificates are issued to ·22 owners only on condition that the rifle is used on approved ranges. Non-compliance with this condition will render the rifleman liable to prosecution under the Firearms Act 1937.

For most shooting of pigeon in trees the rifleman will find, contrary to usual sporting teaching, that the heavier target rifle is a better proposition than the lighter, less accurate, sporting rifle.

Modern air rifles, especially in ·22 calibre, are capable of killing pigeon up to fifty yards (45·5 m) if these birds are hit in the head (as they should be). The older pneumatic guns, which utilize a compressed air reservoir, in calibres of ·25 inch (6·4 mm) and even ·360 inch (9 mm) were capable of killing much larger creatures, including buck, at up to eighty yards (73 m.).

The technique of using miniature rifles and air rifles against pigeons is the subject of a later chapter.

The idea of using a repeating weapon on game is repellent to the true sportsman: certainly the notion of using an automatic shotgun against wildfowl, especially if it means emptying a magazine into some unfortunate flock, or a succession of shots at a bird which, having evaded the legitimate couple of rounds, is entitled to its escape. The automatic weapon and the pump action repeater depend, for *sporting* shooting, on the shooter himself. All too often is it used by the trigger-happy lout who needs must empty his magazine without regard to sporting custom or the unwritten laws of chivalry towards the quarry. From time to time the automatic sporting gun is contrasted with the use of a pair of guns and a loader: at first sight there appears to be some substance in the argument, but consideration will show that there is no true comparison between the two methods.

For pigeon shooting, however, as well as out and out vermin destruction, there is a lot to be said in favour of an automatic or repeating weapon. If the main idea is to combine sport with an agricultural service, then the man who is armed in such a manner that he has the chance of killing more pigeon in a shorter time is obviously worth more to the agricultural community than the man who kills less in the same period. There are many moments, especially when decoying pigeon, when birds fill the air around, the shooter. He fires two shots, manages to slip a third cartridge into the chamber and takes another shot, often hurriedly, and then the chance has gone. It is often suggested that a man could kill five birds with five successive shots with these guns, but I have yet to see a man kill five pigeons with five successive shots, each individually aimed, by means of an automatic gun, and *repeat this performance time and time again.* This would be shooting of a very high order. Perhaps once or twice the feat, for such it would be, may be accomplished two or three times in a season, certainly not more. The most I have seen a shooter pull down with his automatic was four pigeons, all dead in the air at the same time – his first shot was the only miss. It was a wonderful sight – but, so far as I know, that sportsman has never repeated it.

The automatic shotgun, as well as the pump action shotgun, are in popular use in the United States for field as well as clay-pigeon shooting. Excellent guns of this type may be seen at British Clay-pigeon meetings, the most popular model being the semi-automatic.

If the pigeon shooter fancies a repeating shotgun, there is no earthly sporting reason why he should not avail himself of such a weapon and the following brief notes may be of assistance to him in making his choice, double-gun, single-loader, or repeater.

The repeating shotgun was an American invention and today has reached a very high degree of perfection in that country. Repeating shotguns are divided into three main sections:

(*a*) Pump action guns,

(*b*) Self-loading guns, and

(*c*) Bolt-action magazine guns.

The pump action gun is also known as the trombone-action, because the ejection of the fired case and the reloading of the fresh cartridge into the chamber is accomplished by drawing back with the left hand a slide under the gun barrel, rather reminiscent of the musical instrument from which it derived its name. The self-loading gun eliminates the manual work in loading the weapon, while the bolt-action shotguns are operated, as their name suggests, on the same principle as the service rifle, the cartridges being carried in a box magazine.

At first thought the self-loading gun would appear to be the fastest in action, but it is the considered opinion of American authorities, who have far greater experience with this weapon that we are ever likely to have in Britain, that the pump action is the best. The trombone or slide handle is pulled back while the gun is in recoil with the result that the weapon is pulled down out of recoil and aimed at the next target as the slide is pushed forward. The very action of pushing the hand forward helps a correct alingment on to new target.

The bolt-action gun is much slower in action than either of the above and certainly has no advantage over the ordinary shotgun. Great trouble has been experienced in the past with continual breaking of the extractor heads in this type of shotgun, particularly on the German and other Continental models.

The advantages of the repeating shotgun are that the shooter can carry up to five shots in the magazine, can get off a series of shots very quickly, and can operate the gun, if he wishes, as a single loader. What are the disadvantages? Firstly, no matter how well made it may be the repeating shotgun, compared with the standard double or single, is a clumsy piece of work. The overall length is much greater, and this alone is a great disadvantage when shooting from a hide. The great advantage that short barrels give in assisting a sportsman to shoot and swing more easily are lost with the extra length of action of the repeater. The repeating gun is more liable to go out of action than the ordinary shotgun. Wet weather or muddy or sandy conditions may all cause jams and the complicated mechanism is subject to damage.

If a shooter desires to carry two different sizes of shot about with him, say 4's for the left barrel and 6's for the right, he is at a great disadvantage with the repeater as he must use one shot size only.

One often reads about shifting balance and change of weight in an automatic affecting a shooter. Theory, as usual, clashes with practice. Experienced users of repeating weapons have stressed to me, repeatedly, that this may be discounted. All that matters is that a man should be used to his gun.

It may seem peculiar that in this Atomic Age sportsmen should still use muzzle-loading weapons, but a surprisingly large number are in use, ranging from rusty, ill-kept, dangerous pieces in remote rural districts, to the well cared for, safe, high-grade weapons used by collector-sportsmen.

Whatever weapon the sportsman uses ultimately, whether a brand new gun specially acquired for pigeon shooting, or an old favourite used for many years, need I add that it should receive the utmost care and attention in cleaning and maintenance? Let the sportsman remember that it is not the *use* of a gun which shortens its life, but how it is either cared for or neglected when not in use.

At the end of a sporting day the duties of the shooter are firstly to his dog, secondly to his gun. Only when these have been cared for, should he attend to himself.

Finally, no matter how tempting it may be to take a chance shot which might involve an element of danger to some innocent third party or another person's property – such as shooting into cover at an object which cannot be properly identified – always observe the simple, fundamental safety rules. These have been set out so often that there is no point in my repeating them. What I want to do is draw the attention of the sportsman to their very necessity. All guns are lethal weapons, that is their proper function: the sport of shooting pigeon, especially in communal shoots, may sometimes result in accidental injury to either a shooter or shoot servant. The simple rules to prevent such an occurrence. which should be embedded in every shooter's mind, are: Keep cool, do not point your gun, wittingly or unwittingly, at any other object except the bird or animal you intend to kill, and maintain your gun and cartridges in an efficient, safe, and aesthetically pleasing condition.

CHAPTER 4

# *Powder and Shot*

---

Assuming that the sportsman has decided on his choice of weapon the next important question which arises is that of powder and shot.

Probably more letters have been written to editors of sporting journals and more words bandied in shooting circles over the questions of shot size and powder charges than over any other shooting subject. It is very easy to be dogmatic on these questions; it is also easy to compromise to try and suit all parties. Probably the safest course is to advocate that whatever shot size and powder load the sportsman is used to and has confidence in is the best load for his purposes. In general this is true. There are, however, certain points to be considered in the specialized art of pigeon shooting.

'As to shot, I prefer $1\frac{1}{8}$ oz. (31·9 g) of No. 4; most of your birds will be killed *within* thirty yards, and the pattern of this change is close enough at *that* range; and as pigeons are very tough, especially when their crops are full, No. 4 will drop them dead without the risk of their sloping down at a distance, or fluttering away on the ground to hide under the brushwood.' That was the declared opinion of that great authority, Sir Ralph Payne-Gallwey, in his advice on pigeon shooting. (*Letters to Young Shooters, Letter XXVIII.*)

'For shot we prefer No. 5, but here opinions will differ – as always. Many favour for all shooting a small size, No. 7 for instance, but it seems to us a mistake, not to say unsporting, to "pepper" a strong bird with small shot.' That was the opinion expressed by two modern sportsmen, Messrs. G. K. Yeates and R. N. Winnall in a Chapter on Pigeon Shooting. (*Rough Shooting* (1935).)

The pest officers and the agricultural executive committees made cartridges available to registered *bona fide* pigeon shooters at half-price, such cartridges to be expended, against harmful birds. These cartridges were issued in $2\frac{1}{2}$-inch (65 mm) 12-bore size, as a rule, loaded with 4 shot. To the best of my knowledge, they were not issued in smaller sizes, and a more unsuitable cartridge for the job cannot be imagined.

Remembering that the great majority of sportsmen have been brought up to believe in large-sized shot for pigeons, it is interesting to note the modern tendency amongst experienced sportsmen to use smaller sizes of shot. Personally I use 6's or 7's, the reasons for which I will go into later, but perhaps before discussing the theory of large shot we ought to look at the old pastime of pigeon shooting, i.e. the shooting of live birds released from traps.

Pigeon shooting, or 'trap shooting', attracted to its ranks the greatest shots of the day. Names of sportsmen who accomplished wonderful feats in the field, both at feathered game in these islands and against dangerous game abroad, appear in the lists of competitors at the various clubs which catered for this recreation.

Vast sums of money used to change hands at these meetings and the shooters took care to equip themselves with the very best of guns and ammunition. Only the very best conditioned blue rock-pigeons were used in order to test the skill of the competitor to the utmost. The distance from the shooter to the trap from which the bird was released varied from twenty-one to thirty-one yards (19·2 to 28·3 m) according to the skill and handicap of the competitor: contrast this with the sixteen-yard (14·63 m) rise in modern down-the-line clay-pigeon shooting. Thus it will be seen that the top-flight shots were almost at full range when the bird was released. It is therefore very interesting to see what sizes of shot they used, for it must be remembered that a bird missed, or a bird dropped beyond the boundary, meant points lost and with the points went both money and kudos. *The sizes of shot recommended by the most skilled performers at these specially bred and fast flying birds was No. 7, with occasionally No. 8 in the first barrel!*

In view of the choice expressed by those experts the tendency to use large shot is remarkable. Let us examine the arguments for large shot.

Sir Ralph Payne-Gallwey gives an excellent reason: when the crops of these birds are full they are a tougher proposition. But apart from this what reasons are there advanced? Some claim that the feathers of a pigeon are tough and resistant to small shot, they claim that often a bird is hit, a cloud of feathers knocked out of it, but the bird flies on unharmed. These sportsmen also claim that a bird may be seen to stagger when hit with large shot, but recover in flight and escape.

Finally there is the argument that it is not fair to pepper a strong bird with small shot.

What are the arguments against large shot? Firstly the density of killing pattern in the central portion of the shot circle is much less with large shot than with small shot. As a result of this it is possible, expecially at extreme ranges where the pattern is much thinned, for a bird to escape unscathed through the shot. It is also possible for a bird to be struck, in a non-vital part by the odd large pellet from such a thin pattern and as a result to stagger or waver in flight and then fly on. These thinning patterns may also mean that odd pellets knock out a few feathers without actually touching the body of the bird, like a bullet going through a soldier's pack, or through his battle-dress without touching him physically.

It should be noted that Sir Ralph Payne-Gallwey mentions the range at which most pigeon will be killed as *within* thirty yards as then the '*charge is close enough*': in other words *though he recommends large shot, he also recommends that with large shot the range should be shortened.* Quite a paradox!

The case for smaller shot, sizes 6 and 7, is really quite formidable.

With the smaller sizes of shot a dense pattern is achieved making it almost impossible at ranges up to forty yards (36·58 m) for a pigeon to escape without being hit several times, some at least of the hits being in vital places. The striking energy of four or five small pellets, within range, is greater than that of one much larger pellet, and therefore more likely to be mortal.

At close ranges even smaller shot sizes may be used and at pheasants, grouse, and even mallard, sizes 6 and 7 are used by expert marksmen and true sportsmen with the most gratifying results.

Large shot which wounds birds without killing them, or drops them by breaking a wing, should not be used against pigeon. There is an element of cruelty in using these shot sizes as birds mortally hit will carry on a long way, a mile or even more, before succumbing. The man who uses large shot on pigeons will inevitably find that he loses a lot of hit birds and from this he concludes that the pigeon 'is a tough bird and can carry a lot of heavy shot'. Quick, wary, a first-class sporting proposition, yes: but 'tough' no, for the man who uses sizes 6 or 7 for pigeon shooting is the man who drops his birds dead and very rarely hits his birds and watches them disappear into the distance after shedding clouds of feathers.

The head of the bird or small mammal is the correct target when a shotgun is used. The crack shot will nearly always kill his bird by hitting it in the head and neck, though a few pellets must, in the nature of things, find their way into the body. Now the pigeon has a very small head compared with other sporting birds, certainly a ridiculously small head when compared with his body. To ensure that the head and neck receive their full share of the shot charge it is essential to have a dense shot pattern and this can only be achieved by the use of small shot, or by the incorporation of a heavy choke in the gun barrel, or by firing at a shorter range in the case of large shot. *There is no advantage in using heavy shot at short ranges.*

When the pigeon is feeding on the ground or perched in a tree and a sitting shot is about to be taken, there is a reasonable argument in favour of heavier pellets. In those instances the wings of the birds are closed and the larger pellets have a better chance of cutting through the extra thickness of feathers and reaching vital parts. Small shot, sufficient to kill a bird if striking it in the head, may well not penetrate the layers of feathers and this makes for cleaner kills, as well as being more humane.

Perhaps, at this juncture, it is as well to consider the position from the standpoint of ballistics. Most shots are interested in ballistics and the following tables, though only given as an indication of the merits of various shot sizes, may assist the sportsman in arriving at the conclusion that smaller sizes are best for pigeon shooting.

The terms choke, improved cylinder, in the following passages refer to the degree of constriction in the muzzle of a gun, thereby keeping the shot pattern closer together in flight for longer ranges. A full choke is more constricted or tapered than a half-choke. An improved cylinder boring, though very slightly constricted, is practically a parallel tube. Most game guns are made with a greater amount of choke in the left barrel than in the right.

PATTERN PERCENTAGE

| | | *Percentage of total pellets in charge* | | | |
|---|---|---|---|---|---|
| *Range in Yards* | *Range in Metres* | *True Cylinder* | *Improved Cylinder* | *Half Choke* | *Full Choke* |
| 30 | 27·43 | 60 | 72 | 83 | 100 |
| 35 | 32·00 | 49 | 61 | 71 | 84 |
| 40 | 36·58 | 40 | 50 | 60 | 70 |

Thus it will be seen that at thirty yards (27·43 m) a fully choked gun *should* place the whole of its shot pattern in the killing circle. This circle is defined as the central thirty-inch (762 mm) portion of the pattern. An improved cylinder gun will place 72 per cent of its pellets in the same area.

Let us now compare a standard $2\frac{1}{2}$-inch (65 mm) game cartridge 12-bore loaded with $1\frac{1}{16}$ oz. (30·1 g) shot size 4, with a similar cartridge loaded with size 6's.

In the former cartridge there will be 181 pellets and in the latter 287 – a very large increase.

At thirty yards (27·5 m) a fully choked gun will place the whole of its 181 pellets of No. 4 shot in the thirty-inch (760 mm) circle: at the same distance 287 pellets of No. 6 would be thrown into the same area. At forty yards (36·5 m) the same gun would throw 127 pellets of size 4 into that circle, while no less than 201 pellets of No. 6 would cover the same area. At forty-five yards (41·2m), which is stretching the gun a little – the No. 4 pellets should total 107 pellets: at the same range, 168 pellets of No. 6 would fill the pattern.

The obvious result from these figures is that the bird stands less chance of being hit when No. 4 shot is used at ranges over thirty yards (27·45 m). But here the shooter is handicapping himself because, unless he is a top-flight performer, he is using a full choke. At that range the shot spread is twenty-seven inches (685 mm): with a half-choke the spread would be thirty-two inches (810 mm) and with an improved cylinder boring the shot pattern would cover a circle of thirty-eight inches (965 mm) in diameter. It is easier to hit game at close range with a wider spread than a tight choke – that much is obvious. The use of smaller pellets in a gun enables the sportsman to use a lighter choke and yet achieve the same pellet density as the heavier pellets: he has, therefore, a double chance of success as compared with the user of large pellets in heavily choked guns.

At forty yards (36·5 m) a fully choked gun will place 70 per cent of its shot pattern in the thirty-inch (762 mm) circle – in the case of No. 4 shot this would mean 127 pellets out of a $1\frac{1}{16}$ oz. (30·1 g) load of 181 pellets. At the same range a half-choked gun would place 172 pellets of No. 6 shot out of a $1\frac{1}{16}$ oz. (30·1 g) load of 287 pellets, i.e. 60 per cent of its pattern: while an improved cylinder gun would place 50 per cent of its load of No. 6 or 144 pellets. In both cases a denser pattern than when using No. 4 shot.

The striking energy, i.e. killing power, of larger pellets is greater than that of the smaller ones, but at forty yards (36·5 m), whereas the striking energy of No. 4 pellets is (per individual pellet) 2·66 ft.-lb. (3·61 Joules) the striking energy of No. 6 shot is 1·44 ft.-lb. (1·95 Joules). It has been put forward that for birds up to the size of grouse three pellets each having a striking energy of 0·85 ft.-lb. (1·15 Joules) are sufficient for a clean kill. Taking the two shot sizes given at the extreme sporting range of forty yards (36·5 m), there is nothing to choose in practice between 6's and 4's. Here it is interesting to note that one cartridge manufacturer suggests that for pigeons a shot size of 6, with a load of $1\frac{1}{16}$ oz. (33·7 g) is ideal for pigeon, with a maximum range from a fully choked barrel of fifty yards (45·5 m) and a mean range for all borings of forty-eight yards (44 m). For shorter ranges – and most birds are shot at nearer to twenty-five (22·7 m) than forty yards (36·5 m) – the game load of $1\frac{1}{16}$ oz. (30·1 g) or even 1 oz. (28·3 g) is sufficient.

I have used the grouse as an example because it is slightly heavier than the average wood-pigeon, though the two birds may be considered as equal in size for these sporting purposes. For grouse, however, the same manufacturer suggests the normal game loads, with size 6 shot, for effective shooting up to fifty yards (45·7 m) from a fully choked gun.

As a result of these figures the pigeon shooter will conclude that, using size 6 shot with standard game loads, he will be adequately armed to deal with the 'tough' woodies. With these loadings he may go so far as to acquire a gun with, at the most, half-choke – even improved cylinder if he is going to shoot at close ranges – and thereby improve his chances of successful shots. The combination of small shot with a more open boring will compensate for his lack of skill with the tighter chokes and at the same time result in a higher percentage of cleanly killed birds.

From my own experiences, where I have used muzzle-loading guns loaded with but 1 oz. (28·3 g) of No. 6 shot, I have been able to kill as many as thirty-one pigeon out of a 2 lb. (0·91 kg) pouch of shot – missing only one bird, the last shot of the day. Many of the birds on that occasion were taken at a full thirty-five yards (32 m) yet even with that very open boring I was able to drop them dead, cleanly killed.

It has been suggested that small shot is better because it penetrates the feathers and tissues more easily. 'Compare a nail with a needle' is the cry. This is a false assumption. Heavier shot penetrates better because it is heavier, not because it is smaller in diameter. The clouds of feathers flying from a pigeon are a sure sign of the bad shooting of the sportsman concerned: the bird has been hit by the fringe pellets only. A little straighter holding would have brought the bird down.

My choice of 1 oz. (28·3 g) of shot to be fired from a muzzle-loading gun, and that a 10-bore, may seem a little odd. In actual fact there is a sound reason for it. When pellets are sent down the barrel after being fired from a cartridge, a number of them are squeezed together as the charge enters the barrel through the cone from the chamber. Moreover, no matter how well a cartridge is wadded a certain amount of gases escape past the wadding and power is lost as well as pellets deformed by the heat of the flame. As the pellets go through the choke they are again squeezed together and some of them are misshapen as a result. Because of this a proportion of the pellets fly wide and are useless to the shot charge. With the muzzle-loader the wad is seated firmly on the powder and no burning gases escape past it, there is no cone through which the pellets must pass on their way into the barrel nor is there any constriction at the muzzle causing further deformation of the pellets: in other words a 100 per cent shot load, or almost so, is directed towards the target. A lighter load is therefore possible and means a little less recoil to be contended with at the end of a day's sport.

If the sportsman uses a small bore, such as a 16 or 20 or even ·410, he will require a greater degree of choke in order to achieve pellet density. Many writers have described the ·410 as a dangerous toy. They refuse to consider it as an efficient weapon in the field, though they grant that it may be useful to introduce the young idea, or ladies, to shotgun shooting. In the main, however, they maintain that it is worthless as a sporting weapon.

Dangerous, yes. Any gun can be dangerous if used improperly. A toy? Let us see that point of view as expressed by sportsman-writer, Mr. Thurlow Craigs.

'I have absolutely no use for the ·410 as a game gun,' he says in *Shooter's Delight*, 'because for sporting purposes it is a trivial toy which wounds far more than it kills in average hands, at any range over fifteen yards (13·7 m).'

The key word in this passage is '*average*'. There can be no doubt that for pigeon shooting over decoys, where the range seldom exceeds twenty to twenty-five yards (18·29 – 22·86 m), the little 'toy' is a deadly weapon in the hands of a *first-class* shot. Fully choked, it gives sufficient pattern density to kill pigeons stone dead; and its light report does not scare off incoming birds like that of a larger bore. In support of my argument, based on actual experience, I quote Mr. Elmer Keith, the great American authority on shotguns. He says:

'The real small bore, the 3-inch (75 mm) ·410 and the 28-bore are the guns for the expert, never the novice.' It should be borne in mind, however, that American field conditions differ very much from those in England, and that American shooters prefer, in the main, heavier loads and larger guns for game shooting than we do. If the pigeon shooter is limited to a ·410 gun, let him take heart. If he practises until he can swing and lead properly on his target, he won't be disappointed when he comes to decoy work for the ring-dove. By keeping to short ranges, using expert field-craft and woodmanship to make up for the lack of extra pellets and shooting distance, he will acquit himself well and take his due toll of these wary birds.

On the subject of ·410 shotguns for pigeon shooting, the control of these birds in the London parks is a major problem. To give a typical example, at evening countless thousands of wood-pigeon and feral domestic pigeons flight into Regent's Park to roost on the wooded islands of the boating lake. The feeding of these birds by the general public (and I must confess to being guilty of this myself), attracts many more birds than are economically necessary. It will come as a surprise to many to learn that these birds are controlled by shooting. No doubt this will be a severe blow to the ardent bird-lover protectionist, but the fact is that these pigeons are thinned out regularly, in the early morning, by ·410 shotguns issued to the keepers. If the ·410 were but a toy which wounded more than it killed, the public would soon be kicking up a fuss about winged birds. The ·410 does its job well. Its choice is obvious as its small report does not alarm the birds until execution has been done, and hides from the public the fact that their pets are being killed by shooting.

During 1977, from February until late August, except for one or two sporting days, my shooting of wood-pigeons, and stock-doves, was carried out solely with a ·410 double-barrel shotgun. The cartridges I used were the 2½-inch (65 mm) 'Fourlong' and the shot sizes were 6's and 7's, according to availability in the gunshops. Shooting mostly over decoys, occasionally at roost, my bag was greater than equivalent periods for previous years when I used a standard 12-bore. This in spite of the fact that pigeons were not so numerous in the early part of that year.

Though most of the shooting took place at about twenty-five yards (22·86 m), a few birds were killed cleanly at the normal 12-bore range, i.e. about thirty to thirty-five yards (27·4 – 32 m). In addition to pigeons I used the gun with great effect on rabbits (my shoot being one of the isolated pockets which escaped the scourge of myxomatosis), rooks, grey squirrels, and crows. Although it would be ridiculous to compare the larger bore unfavourably with the ·410 – nevertheless I proved to my own satisfaction, as well as that of shooting friends, that *held straight* and confined to ranges not exceeding thirty to thirty-five yards (27·4 – 32 m) using small sized shot to fill the pattern, the $2\frac{1}{2}$-inch (65 mm) ·410 shotgun is a deadly little weapon. Certainly not the dangerous *toy* some 'authorities' would have us believe.

4. The cartridges give an excellent indication of the capability of the .410 gun compared with a 12-bore, and its limitations.

It is often said that when pigeon are shot as they come in to roost, powerful cartridges in long-chambered guns are an absolute necessity. This is a fallacy. A pigeon which is forty yards high (36·5 m), i.e.

120 feet off the ground, is a veritable skyscraper of a bird and the average shot would not even think of aiming at it, let alone loosing a round at it. It stands to reason, then, that what are normally considered very high birds are within range of the normal game gun and its normal cartridge. For those so-called high birds, shot sizes 6 and 7 are perfectly adequate.

I have often shot these birds and with the greatest confidence. Invariably my companions have remarked about the terrifically high birds I was pulling down. In many instances these were shot with 1 oz. (28·3 g) of No. 7 shot from my muzzle-loader with its very open pattern. In actual fact the birds were considerably less than forty yards in height above me, though my companions took a lot of convincing.

A good way of becoming accustomed to seeing high birds in the proper perspective is to borrow a small box-kite from some young friend or relative. Lay the kite out on the ground with forty yards (36·58 m) of light string attached to it. Note the size it appears and how far away it seems. Then fly the kite into the breeze. Naturally it will not climb immediately overhead and there will be a little bellying of the cord, so that it will be less than forty yards high and slightly nearer the experimenter than the grounded kite. The flying kite will seem much farther away than the grounded article. This optical illusion is particularly in evidence when wing shooting and can only be overcome by constant observation and shooting practice.

To summarize all this: the $2\frac{1}{2}$-inch (65 mm) 12-bore game cartridge, loaded with $1\frac{1}{16}$ (30·1 g) or even 1 oz. (28·3 g) of Number 6 or 7 shot, is perfectly good enough for all forms of pigeon shooting. If a small bore gun is used, the shots must be taken at closer ranges, but, all in all, it may be said that whereas small bores, 16, 20, 28 and even ·410 may be used successfully, it is a waste of gun powder, as well as powder and shot, to employ anything larger than a $2\frac{1}{2}$-inch (65 mm) 12-bore when shooting pigeons.

CHAPTER 5

# *Hides and Blinds*

There are three main types of pigeon shooting:

(*a*) Shooting over decoys.
(*b*) Shooting them at the roost.
(*c*) Flight shooting.

5. A good shooting position. However, though the shooter is wearing camouflaged clothing, the ditch hide does need extra cover. See next photo.

In addition one can stalk and walk up pigeons in the woods or on their feeding grounds. This is very little practised, though it can be thrilling, if unrewarding in numbers of birds bagged.

Unless one stalks the birds from behind cover, or walks them up from tree to tree, the shooter will find it necessary to use hides or blinds from which to take his shots. He may be fortunate enough to make use of natural cover, for example a clump of bushes or a deep ditch or drain, but, by and large, most pigeon shooters have to make use of artificial hides. These may be portable apparatus, permanent structures, or temporary constructions from materials at hand on the site.

6. A deep ditch makes a good hide – but it requires some cover to conceal the shooter. Here netting has been stretched across the ditch and covered with local vegetation.

The building and siting of hides is no hit and miss affair. Much thought must be given to the job, if it is to bring about a successful termination to the forays.

Before commencing the construction of any form of hide, blind, or butt it is essential that the sportsman should get to know, as thoroughly as possible, the land over which he will be shooting. For, of course, the position of these hides will have to be changed several times during the course of a year. The direction of the wind, the rotation of cropping, the agricultural or industrial developments in the environments of the shot, all will from time to time make it necessary for hides to be moved to new positions or for new hides to be erected.

The first factor to be considered is: *Where are the pigeon likely to be, or what are their likely flight lines?* The next, after the former has been resolved, is: *What effect will wind and weather have on the birds? To what extent will their habits be influenced?*

For instance, it may well be that though the pigeon frequent a particular field and the shooter has observed that their direction of approach is generally from one particular point, certain conditions may cause the birds to enter the target area from some other point. If the hide first selected is up against the shoot boundary, it may be impractical to shoot the birds in their new approach lines. The probable solution to such a problem may be to build an alternative hide at the other end of the field.

With the first two questions satisfactorily settled, the next problem will be: *Of what materials should the hide be constructed and how should it be placed?*

If there is a hedge, clump of bushes, small wood, or deep ditch available the answer is straightforward, but a major problem will arise where a field is, for instance, very large, or where the boundaries to the field consist solely of wire fences and there is no ditch. Obviously a hide cannot be built out of harmony with the surroundings, for it will then stand out as a strange and, therefore, dangerous object to the pigeons. Nor is it advisable to erect a portable structure there and then. If there are no local materials, which can be converted into a hide, immediately available, then the question of digging pits must be considered.

On the digging of pits – indeed on the construction of any type of hide which is permanent in form – the landowner or farmer should be consulted before any steps are taken to carry out the scheme. A pit wrongly placed, positioned without the farmer's consent, may result in damage to livestock or farming machinery. Very few farmers will object to proper shooting pits being dug for the purpose of shooting the grey-blue marauders, but two conditions must be fulfilled by the shooter who undertakes such work.

1. He should take care to warn all farm servants and others likely to be in the vicinity of the pit that a hole has been excavated into which they might fall and injure themselves, and
2. Provide an adequate cover or lid to the pit to minimize the likelihood of anyone falling into it. This also has the advantage of keeping the interior of the pit dry in wet weather. There is nothing more disconcerting than having to bale out many buckets of water before shooting or trying to shoot with feet embedded in sticky mud or clay.

If the pit is not near the fence, but in the open field, it is fairly easy to protect livestock by putting four posts round it, suitably wired. These posts need only be two feet (0·6 m) in height and their presence will not alarm the pigeons.

7. A hedge or bush makes a good base for a hide.

There are occasions when hides can be thrown together from materials temporarily on the site in order to come to terms with

8. Bales of hay or straw make an excellent hide.

pigeons which are frequenting the scene for a limited period only. For example, when hay has been cut, or when the straw is baled, the sportsman can use the bundles, cocks, stooks, or whatever is present. I have in mind such an occasion when shooting over a friend's shoot practically in London. The pigeon were feeding on the peas during the morning and late afternoon, when the workers were not gathering them. Scattered about the pea field were large numbers of wooden boxes into which the peas were collected. A very effective hide was made by building up a few of these boxes into a small hut. The very fact that there were several scores of these boxes about seemed to blind the pigeon to the fact that two unusually large piles of boxes had been erected in the middle of the field. The birds came in to the peas, swinging in to the decoys, in spite of the shots poured into them. There was a continuous passage of pigeons which often flew within a few feet of these home-made, clumsy, but withal very efficient hides.

Before, therefore, going into the question of building special hides, it is advisable to group them into their various categories, which are:

(*a*) Temporary hides, and

(*b*) Permanent hides.

Temporary hides are divided into further categories. (1) Hides constructed of natural materials, such as grasses, branches of trees, small bushes, etc., in the immediate vicinity of the shooting area and (2) Hides constructed of artificial or manufactured materials either already on the site or brought thereto.

9. Interior of bale hide.

Permanent hides may be divided into two main classes (1) Surface hides and pits, and (2) Elevated hides or *machans*. The *machan* is too often neglected in England. In Scotland, where pigeon shooting is appreciated on many of the sporting estates, being specially catered for after game shooting ends, and where the 'doo' is promoted almost to the position of game, elevated hides built into trees or high bushes are not uncommon. Particularly when shooting a roost at evening a hide built into a tree or tall bush will give the gunner many more sporting opportunities than will come to him when shooting from ground level. The *machan* reduces the range at which he is shooting, and from it the shooter will often get a clearer idea of where a dead bird falls.

But all forms of hide must conform to the following requirements:

1. They must form part of the natural background.
2. They must be unobtrusive.
3. They must be large enough for the shooter to be comfortable.
4. There must be sufficient room for the gun to be swung freely.
5. They should be sufficiently high *all round* to give perfect concealment.
6. The *floor* of the hide should be level.
7. Wherever possible the hide should have its back to the sun.

The tools required for construction of an artificial hide, or for the conversion of natural cover are simple and few in number. A sharp knife, some stout twine, a few short lengths of galvanized wire, perhaps a bill-hook, are all that are necessary. For the construction of permanent hides, especially the *machan* or platform hide, a hammer and nails, and a small saw will probably also be necessary.

For the purpose of this book, however, I propose to treat the construction of hides under the following headings:

(*a*) Temporary hides.
(*b*) Permanent hides.
(*c*) Portable hides.

## *Temporary Hides*

Some examples of these have been given, viz. the use of hay bales and pea boxes. It is also possible to shoot pigeon from pieces of farm equipment and machinery which have been left on the site. The birds are used to these objects and do not seem to fly wide of them. I have often taken successful shots over a long period when only partly hidden behind a plough. Portable arks or poultry houses are often ideal for this work and a piece of sacking stretched between two sticks or canes behind the gunner often gives sufficient concealment.

Pea netting stretched along a hedge, with further lengths of this material brought round three or four sticks so that it forms a semi-circle round the rear of the shooter, the whole festooned with pieces of grass, rushes, small branches of the local vegetation, makes an excellent temporary structure.

Three or four small bushes, with the centre branches lopped out, generally make a comfortable shooting spot.

10. Netting stretched between two bushes – prior to festooning with local materials.

11. Completely covered hide with netting base.

Shooting in woodlands in autumn, it is possible to build up a mound of bracken, undergrowth and dead twigs, in the midst of which the shooter may conceal himself. If the whole is liberally covered with fallen leaves it makes a capital blind.

If the shoot is bounded by stone walls, as in the North, a piece of sacking will give adequate cover and is not conspicuous.

One simple temporary structure may be made by cutting three or four sticks which are placed in the ground. String is run along these, and branches or grasses woven in and out of the twine. The structure should not be made too solid however, only sufficient to break up the outlines of the shooter and conceal any movements he may make. If using branches with leaves it is important that the leaves should face *outward*. In summer it may be necessary to replenish the greenery once or more times during the day as the foliage may droop alarmingly and will then appear most unconvincing.

Pigeons are apt to lose their wariness in the presence of mechanical vehicles. Quite often a friend and I used to shoot a long avenue of beeches which lined the drive leading up to a large country residence. It was impossible to stalk or walk up the birds in the trees: it was impractical (for reasons which need not be gone into here) to place decoys near by to entice them into the open. But the birds afforded comparatively easy shooting from a moving motor-car. Our method was to roll slowly along the drive. I stood up in the car on the front seat with my gun at the ready, poking up through the open sunshine roof like a tank commander on a victory parade. But such shooting is now illegal under the Protection of Birds Act, 1954.

It is possible, however, to drive a vehicle on to a field where pigeon feed, and then park the car, van, tractor, or whatever it is and wait for the birds to come in. Used this way, as a *static* hide, one can have adequate sport for a short time.

### *Permanent Hides*

These are sited where birds are likely to be met with regularly. If a permanent hide takes the form of a pit, it should be at least 4 ft. 6 in. (1·3 m) in depth and 2 ft. 6 in. (0·75 m) or 3 ft. (0·9 m) square, or 3 ft. (0·91 m) in diameter if circular. The taller the shooter, the deeper the pit, of course. The earth which is thrown up from the pit should be spread out over the surrounding area, though a little bank, not more than 6 inches (150 mm) in height is permissible round the hole.

This bank should be smoothed down so that it merges, imperceptibly, into the ground surface. To improve the pit, a couple of posts, with a length of cord between them, extending up to 2 feet (0·6 m) above the pit, may be inserted before and removed after shooting. From these posts a length of camouflage netting, or other material, suitably garnished with local foliage, will be extended back from the hide and pegged into the ground. The ângle of the netting, which should spread out to the sides as well as the rear, should be a slight incline. The object of this netting, which should extend about half-way over the pit is to provide a roof which will hide the shooter from birds approaching from his rear: at the same time, the nature of this 'roof', net and vegetation, allows the gunner to observe approaching birds.

A permanent hide may be constructed by setting six to eight posts (standard rose posts are ideal) into the ground. These should be about 6 inches (150 mm) apart and the crevices stuffed with hay, hedge trimmings, straw, pine boughs and so on. Such a butt, needless to say, should be placed in front of a natural hedge, or in front of a wood. They make ideal hides from which to shoot roosting pigeon, and a whole series of them may be constructed along the shoot hedges to suit the various conditions under which the pigeons may be encountered.

In covert, bundles of boughs may be gathered together and wired to form a hut, with an open top, about 6 feet (1·8 m) or more in height. These are best situated in a clearing on the flight line. The addition of a little roof over one corner will provide extra concealment from above as well as a little shelter in inclement weather.

Permanent structures of wood stakes, even galvanized iron stakes set into hedges, with strands of wire round them, or covered with wire netting, make excellent frameworks for these covert hides. They should be hung with local vegetation, which should be renewed frequently, as in the case of temporary hides.

Derelict farm structures, old drinking troughs, and so forth can form the basis for permanent hides. I made excellent use of an old drinking trough on one shoot. It would have been useless to have tried to shoot pigeons from it in its form as a trough. However, there was a disused water-pump at one end which had, at one time, had a timber 'sleeve' around it. I therefore built a timber cupboard at the end of the trough, utilizing this 'sleeve' as the basis of the design. I made the shelter high enough and wide enough to conceal myself, and after completing the work by giving it a coat of creosote left it unoccupied for several weeks to allow the pigeons to become accustomed to the new object on their feeding ground. I shot from this hide over decoys and had a fair amount of success though the narrowness of the trough itself did militate against quick-manoeuvring of the body into different positions when birds came in from unexpected angles.

In this connection, I should add that on windless days I have found pigeon coming in to decoys from every point of the compass. In such circumstances it is essential to be able to change position rapidly if excellent chances are not to be lost. In the field it always seems that the chances which are lost are the best chances of all. How many times will the shooter hear others declair——'If only——': indeed, he will often be given to that sad phrase himself when running over the day's events. 'If only——' is the epitaph of missed opportunity.

When constructing platform hides or *machans* as they are sometimes termed, considerably more carpentry is required. The hide must be sited in such a position that the shooter will be able to have a clear field of fire, and yet placed so that it does not attract the attention of the birds. Moreover, it must be sturdy enough to take the weight of a sportsman, who may weigh anything from about 140 lb. (63 kg) to over 200 lb. (90 kg). Stout timbers are necessary for the floor frame, and these can be covered with tongued and grooved planks, or tree backs. Timber floors can be very treacherous to stand upon when wet and it is a sound practice to give them a good coat of pitch and to throw plenty of sand, gravel, cinders, etc., upon the hot pitch in order to provide a rough surface. A stout guard rail should surround the platform and on this, with a suitable aperture for the shooter to climb through, branches and netting should be fixed to complete the blind. Strong though it must be, a platform hide must not have a solid appearance.

The fork in a tree makes an ideal site for a platform hide, but better by far are the methods I saw adopted on one sporting estate in Inverness-shire. This was the fixing of the hide amongst four young larch trees. They were utilized to form the girders of the structure. This method minimizes the amount of movement to which platform hides are subject on windy days, and also makes for a more secure perch from which to shoot.

Do not nail your platform to the tree. Firstly, the driving of large nails into a tree is detrimental to the growing timber. Secondly, nails are subject to rusting and liable to break, and the consequences of that could be disastrous. It is better to fix the platform by means of scaffolding ropes which have been treated with creosote. There is a certain amount of elasticity in this method which, though the whole structure may creak and groan ominously in a high wind, by its very 'give' lowers the chance of a collapsed hide. When fastened by nails or spikes the rigid structure, under wind stress, is apt to split the wooden frame of the platform.

Until one gets used to the feeling, shooting from a platform hide, about twenty feet (6 m) from the ground, in half a gale is an unnerving experience. The whole structure heaves to and fro, accompanied by the queerest sounds. What happened to the unfortunate baby in the tree-top cradle when the wind blew must, inevitably, cross the sportsman's mind. However, one soon becomes accustomed to it and learns to anticipate the sway which otherwise can ruin a perfectly good shot at an easy bird. A ladder is, of course, an essential for this type of hide.

Platform hides may also be constructed in tall bushes, where the problem is not nearly so great. If a hide is built in such a position it is often only necessary to make a platform and guard rail. Keep the interior branches well cut back but allow the exterior branches to grow. In one season such a hide becomes the most perfect of all: it looks natural, provides perfect cover, and *is* natural.

The question of whether or not any hide should have a roof, must depend upon the taste of the individual shooter. The average shot generally prefers an open-top hide for the simple reason that this allows him a variety of sporting shots which may be taken at all angles and heights. A compromise may be achieved by laying a branch across the top of the hide: this will partly conceal the shooter. Another effective way of providing top cover, yet allowing for the chance of taking varied shots, is to construct the hide on the lines of the Red Indian wigwam, i.e. with the walls sloping in towards the top.

The professional pigeon-shot, or the man who is desirous of getting as many pigeons as possible cleared off the shoot, or the man who simply wishes to get a good average of kills for cartridges expended, generally prefers a closed-top hide. Such a hide has to be built with small windows in the sides, through which shots can be taken, or like a battlemented tower with a roof added. It is an advantage, too, to have a small opening in the roof to allow for tree shots.

The third category of hides is the portable hide or blind. It is possible to buy ready made hides, but these are often bulky as well as being expensive. For portable hides the shooter has many materials to choose from. He may use camouflage netting, obtainable at many army surplus stores, and with four or more stakes to which it can be fastened, has an easily erected blind. But camouflage nets can be bulky and heavy.

Wire galvanised chicken netting makes a good base for a portable hide – it is light, tough, but not easy to work with.

A material I have found excellent is the Netlon material used by gardeners. This is available in different meshes – the smaller the better for pigeon shooting purposes. It is obtainable from most garden centres and ironmongers and its price varies according to its width.

It is available in three colours, white, green, and brown. Personally I prefer the brown because it will fit in with most backgrounds: the white I had considered for snow shooting, but haven't experimented in that direction yet. But Netlon, and similar materials are very light in weight, roll into a small space when being transported, and being plastic are virtually indestructible. They can be hosed or scrubbed down to get them clean and will last for many seasons. Material from site is easily attached to them, and I very strongly recommend this material for the serious pigeon shooter. If ever you have tried to carry, gun, cartridges, and a camouflage net whilst riding a bicycle, you will soon appreciate the lightweight and compactness of the Netlon alternative.

Finally, of all positions in which a hide should be sited, the best, by far, is in the vicinity of a *dead* tree. Most pigeons prefer to settle in a dead tree when making their spy-out of the terrain prior to feeding. If lofted decoys are used, of which more in the following chapter, a dead tree enables the decoy to be more easily seen by the birds. Furthermore, the absence of leaves makes it easier for a sportsman to take tree shots successfully.

The hide in itself is not sufficient. The hide is merely a curtain between the sportsman and the birds, and it is an absolute essential that the gunner should avoid all unnecessary movements while in the hide. The top of a sportsman's head, with or without headgear, is visible to the birds long before the sportsman himself has got his eyes over the edge! Nothing is more destructive of camouflage, however perfect, than movement. The golden rule is, therefore, *absolute stillness*.

Clothing should be suited to the colouration of the general

surroundings: certainly yellow pullovers and bright checks are out! Grey and fawn are the best colours, and there is no harm in using camouflage clothing. A trilby, a deerstalker or peaked cap is best for shooting headgear, since they partly conceal the face. A trilby is better than a cap, because in wet weather it prevents water dripping down the shooter's neck, a most uncomfortable experience which detracts from good shooting.

Pigeons have exceptionally keen eyesight, far better, apparently, than their hearing and they are quick to see anything which might spell danger to them. The most conspicuous objects seen lurking in or behind most hides (and it is surprising how many shooters are given away to the birds by these) are the human hands and the human face, particularly the latter! Some shooters wear masks and veils. Personally I have found by experience that these can be rather a nuisance. If the shoot is, as many are, infested with countless myriads of hungry midges, it may afford some protection from their attacks, but heaven help the sportsman should the midges find an entrance.

The camouflaging of the face and hands may be done by the use of burnt cork, as Commando soldiers and paratroops did on operations, or by simply rubbing mud or earth over them. Mittens may be used for the hands. Gloves are an abomination and make for dangerous handling of the gun, particularly if it is a hammer weapon. And it is not too easy to pick up and place cartridges into the breech if you are wearing gloves.

Do not stint labour. Construct as many hides as possible on the shoot, particularly if it be near a roost. There is no great expense involved in the construction of even the most elaborate hide. I know of one sportsman who, shooting pigeons in mid-winter, constructed a first-class hide. It was a pit dug into the side of a mound, lined with timber and roofed. He made a seat, provided hooks from which he could hang his equipment and decoys and installed an oil stove! There is no need to go as far as that but no hide, however constructed, is of any use to the sportsman if it is uncomfortable, or cramped. No hide for that matter is of the slightest use if, though perfectly built, embodying all the refinements the craftsman can imagine, it is placed on the wrong site.

Prior observation coupled with common sense are the two basic essentials in hide building.

CHAPTER 6

# *Decoys*

It is a fairly safe assumption that the great majority of pigeons shot in this country are killed over decoys. Decoys are dummy birds which are set up to imitate feeding or resting pigeons. Their use may mean pigeons brought to bag which would otherwise pass unscathed. But they must be used intelligently, and under the proper conditions, for wrongly used they will serve only to scare the pigeons off.

Before considering the conditions under which decoys should be used and the methods of shooting over them, it will be as well to examine their purpose, the different types and the methods of construction.

Pigeons being wild, cunning, and wary have learnt to distinguish between the man in the city, who is benevolent and given to feeding them, who at worst merely ignores them, and the man in the countryside who is their eternal enemy, constantly striving to reduce their numbers. Pigeons, too, seem to be able to distinguish between the worker in the fields, and the same person in the same surroundings bent on their destruction. 'They know a man with a gun,' is a common sporting expression, denoting that the birds would not let the sportsman get within gunshot. Now this very wariness, this fear of human beings in the countryside, can be used to lure the pigeons (and wildfowl and corvidae, too, for that matter) to their doom. If these fearful creatures see their companions feeding peacefully on certain grounds, or sitting at ease resting, they may well assume that it is perfectly safe for them to join in. Decoys form the basis of this illusion. The birds see what are, apparently, their companions. If a bird reasons, it must consider that the area is safe – otherwise their comrades would not be there – and so attempts to join them. The decoys are carefully placed in a natural manner ('setting out' is the correct term) well within range of the sportsman who is thus enabled to take comparatively easy shots at his quarry. Shooting over the decoys does not seem to trouble the birds unduly as they will continue to come in to the decoys despite the disturbance.

The first and foremost rule in the use of decoys is that they must be placed in a natural manner. It matters not if the sportsman has a score of the most beautifully made decoys, or even mounted birds, if his setting out of them is faulty. Better poor decoys in a perfect layout.

Spring and early summer are the best times of the year for effective use of decoys as at that time the birds are not yet gathered together in large flocks. Decoys may, however, be used all round the year. In many cases they are the deciding factor, if placed in the tops of the tall trees to which birds are flighting, between a successful roost shoot and a failure.

12. A natural decoy, a recently shot pigeon, set in position by means of a short stick into the ground and through the crop into the neck

Beyond all doubt the best decoys, though rather fragile for average use, and certainly much too expensive for the man with a limited income, are stuffed, mounted birds. The present-day cost of taxidermy, however, places this type of decoy in the luxury class of goods. The next best decoy is a bird which the sportsman has just shot. It is quite easy to set such a bird up in a lifelike manner, the only requisites being some galvanized wire or a small diamond of wire netting, or (as a makeshift) a forked twig, or thin stick. The length of the wire or stick will depend upon the height of the vegetation or crops upon which the pigeons are feeding and where the decoys are to be placed. It is a golden rule that decoys should be placed on the top of the vegetation or crops. Naturally, if feeding on loose corn seeds, the decoy will be set up on the ground; if feeding on clover or brassicas, the stick will have to be much longer. If a piece of wire or sharp stick is used, one end is stuck into the pigeon's head from below. The other end is pressed into the ground with the body of the dead bird supported (to leg height) with whatever materials, soil, stubble, etc., are at hand. If the small diamond-shaped piece of wire netting is used, this is folded round the underside of the bird's body, with the neck placed in a natural position and supported by the mesh: a piece of wire can then be introduced into the wire netting and the lower end of it pressed into the ground. Wire netting is very useful when it is desired to use recently shot birds as lofted decoys.

If the sportsman has neither wire netting nor pieces of wire in his haversack, then he may use small forked twigs, sharpened at the base end. The pigeon is supported on a couple of such twigs: a longer, finer twig supporting the neck and head, a shorter, stouter twig supporting the body immediately in front of the leg. The ends of these twigs should be pressed into the ground.

'First catch your hare,' is the cliché attributed to the late Mrs. Beeton of culinary fame: the average pigeon shot may well find that 'first shoot your pigeon' is an even greater obstacle!

Some professional pigeon shooters advocate that the eyelid of the dead bird should be cut off, in order that the decoys may look lifelike. In actual practice I have not found this to be necessary. Most decoys will often be set out at ranges varying from twenty to thirty yards (18·3 to 27·4 m) from the sportsman. If pigeons, coming in to decoys, get close enough to see whether the set-up birds have their eyes closed or not, they are certainly near enough for the shooter to kill their curiosity. It is the same with hand-carved, painted decoys of pigeon and wildfowl. The extra refinements, the wonderful feathering effects, the glass eyes, do not seem to make the slightest difference to the incoming birds. I firmly believe that the removal of the eye-lid from the dead bird, and the fitting of glass eyes into decoys, are on a par with the painting of eyes *et cetera* on Devon Minnows and other spinning lures – gratifying to the craftsman but of little or no use in practice.

The next decoy to be considered is the carved and painted bird. These are particularly good for lofted decoys in trees and have the great merit of being life-like and long-lasting. The one great objection which has been made against them is that a dozen solid decoys are heavy to carry about. I agree with this view, though I think that it is more often founded on hearsay than experience. If the pigeon shooter has access to shooting grounds it may logically be assumed that it will be easy for him to come to arrangements with the farmer to leave the decoys at the farm or in the farm buildings. They can then be picked up and taken out on to the shoot as and when required and the problem of porterage of heavy, bulky articles will not arise. Furthermore, unless one has reason to doubt the honesty of the local inhabitants, or unless the shooting ground is likely to be the playground of irresponsible youths or poachers, there is no reason why the decoys should not be cached in a box in one of the permanent hides.

In addition to the carved wooden decoys, there are now on the market some very excellent hand-painted life-like rubber decoys. Some models of this type are mounted on a coiled spring which causes them to move with the least vibration or wind, and this continual movement makes a very realistic 'field'. There are other rubber models of pigeon on the market which are collapsible and self-inflating. They pack easily into a pocket, are tough and long-lasting, and very life-like. They should last many seasons, so that, though the initial cost may seem a little high, it will be found at the end of the season that they were a cheap purchase.

Another type of decoy is of papier mâché, hollow, and generally with a detachable head. These are light in weight, easily transportable, look every bit as realistic as the rubber and solid wood types, but have the advantage that the heads may be set in variable postures. These decoys stack into each other for ease in carrying, and are set up on a slotted wooden peg. It should be remembered, however, that they will not suffer the rough handling that the other types will stand up to without damage.

There is also the semi-silhouette type of decoy. The most famous of these is that designed by that great pigeon shot, Max Baker, and known as the Max Baker Decoy. This is probably the most popular of all forms of wood-pigeon decoys. It consists of a flat, compressed paper body, covered with canvas and painted to imitate a wood-pigeon. The sides of the body are made by simply curving the decoy in the hand. It is set up on a double-spiked steel pin, head to wind, and, in consequence, moves in the slightest breeze, thereby giving the impression of a feeding bird. Unfortunately, however, it does not always keep head to wind and in gusty weather may be blown off the peg. There have been several models brought out on Max Baker lines, each incorporating various improvements, generally in the fixing of the decoy on the peg. Some of these decoys are made of other materials than compressed paper and canvas: for example, stamped out of sheet aluminium and hand-painted. It is safe to state that most decoys which are made at home by the sportsman are fashioned on the Max Baker lines.

Finally, there are the true silhouette decoys, made from sheet metal, plywood, cardboard, or thin wood, and shaped to give the appearance of a pigeon either feeding or resting, when viewed from the side. If used alone, they are not very successful: they can, however, be used as lofted decoys in trees and bushes, and also placed in a 'field' of other types of decoys to increase the numbers.

It will be seen that the sportsman has plenty of types from which to choose. They vary in style, portability, and price, but the keen shot will soon discover one great failing common to all manufactured decoys. All proprietary types of decoy are *painted to represent adult wood-pigeons only*. I believe this to be a great mistake – just as great a mistake as it would be to set out a field of drake mallards when wild-fowling. I have found by long experience that pigeons will come in to decoys better if young birds are imitated; that is, birds without the white neck collar. Furthermore, the addition of one or two stock-dove decoys is essential if the sportsman is going to have a full set of proper equipment. When setting out decoys I have added one or two Max Baker types of my own manufacture, painted to simulate domestic pigeon; plenty of brown in the 'plumage', no white collars, mottled white-grey plumage, and so forth. The result, in the way of the extra shooting which has come my way, has been amazing.

When choosing decoys for lofting, the shooter will find that solid wood decoys are probably the best. Mounted on lofting poles (long poles joined together by male and female ferrules like fishing rods) and thrust up into tall trees or bushes, these decoys bring pigeons in when ground decoys are achieving nothing. A decoy, should have a vane under the tail in order to keep the bird head to wind and a couple of hooks, one on top and one underneath the body, to which cords are attached. A weighted cord is thrown over a branch by means of a stick or from a catapult, and the decoy is raised on this cord to the required position.

13. Lofting a decoy by means of a cord cast over a branch.

Recently killed birds, when rolled in wire netting, can also be raised in this manner. The cord is fastened to a loop of the netting over the back of the bird, the other cord is fastened to the underside and the bird raised to the required position. Alternatively, the bird may be fastened to a wire fork on the top of the lofting pole, which is then lifted to the proper height.

Pigeons will come in more readily to decoys which move. The use of live birds for decoying though very popular on the Continent is illegal in Great Britain. Mechanical moving decoys, which flapped their wings, once on the market are, at the moment of writing, unobtainable. Their mechanism was simple. They were operated electrically, and the current was taken from a small dry-cell type battery. Hidden in his butt or shooting pit all the sportsman had to do to attract the attention of pigeons in the vicinity was to press a button. He could thus make the mechanical bird 'perform' at will.

14. Adjusting the wings of the Cogswell & Harrison decoy.

The nearest approach to a mechanical decoy on the British market at the present day is one which though strictly speaking is not mechanically operated, nevertheless is fitted with a pair of wings which flap! These decoys introduced by Cogswell and Harrison consist merely of a pair of rubber wings with flexible wire supports. These wings are attached to the standard rubber decoy pigeon and

15. Adjusting the wings of the Cogswell & Harrison decoy.

when correctly positioned the bobbing about of the decoy in the wind causes the wings to flap. This decoy can also be operated by means of a length of line attached to the rear and passed through an eye on the mounting peg. By pulling on the cord the shooter can make the decoy rock and so flap the rubber wings. An ideal moment to 'flap' is when pigeons are still out of range: the movement usually lures them in to make a closer inspection.

Much amusement may be had by making one's own decoys. There is a lot of pleasure in using decoys one has manufactured by oneself. But it may well be that the carving of solid wood decoys is beyond the capabilities of the average sportsman and he has to consider something easier. Suppose, therefore, that we consider the manufacture of the Max Baker type of decoy.

The necessary tools are a pair of stout scissors, tinsnips, some paint, a paint brush and a pair of pliers. The materials required will be either sheet cardboard, sheet metal, thin plywood (marine quality), some dowelling, a little wire, some panel pins, pumice stone, and black and white and green paint.

These decoys are of two types, still and moving.

### *Still Decoys*

Whatever material the craftsman works with, be it sheet metal or cardboard, he must cut it into sheets 15 inches by 12 inches (380 by 305 mm) for each decoy. If cardboard is used it should be sufficiently thin to roll into a 3 inch (75 mm) diameter cylinder without cracking. Much material can be obtained from old cartons and boxes. For stock-dove decoys, which are slightly smaller, two decoys can be made from the average shoe box. The first requirement is a suitable template or pattern. This is made by drawing a series of one-inch squares on one of the sheets of material. Using the inch squares (25·4 mm) as a guide draw the pattern outline as shown in Fig. 16A.

Cut out the sketch. This can now be used as a template to mark out the others. Simply lay the pattern on the flat sheets of material and draw round it with a soft pencil. The shaded portions on the side flaps of the pattern are bent inwards and glued over and under each other when the decoy receives its final shape. It will be noted that the shaded portion is set at a slant: this slant must be maintained if a correct shape is to be given to the decoy which, in its completed form, tapers towards the tail. In this manner the decoys may be stacked inside each other for carrying.

When sufficient decoys have been marked out (ten to twelve may be regarded as an absolute minimum), take the first decoy in the hands and bend the sides inward until the shaded portions of the flap

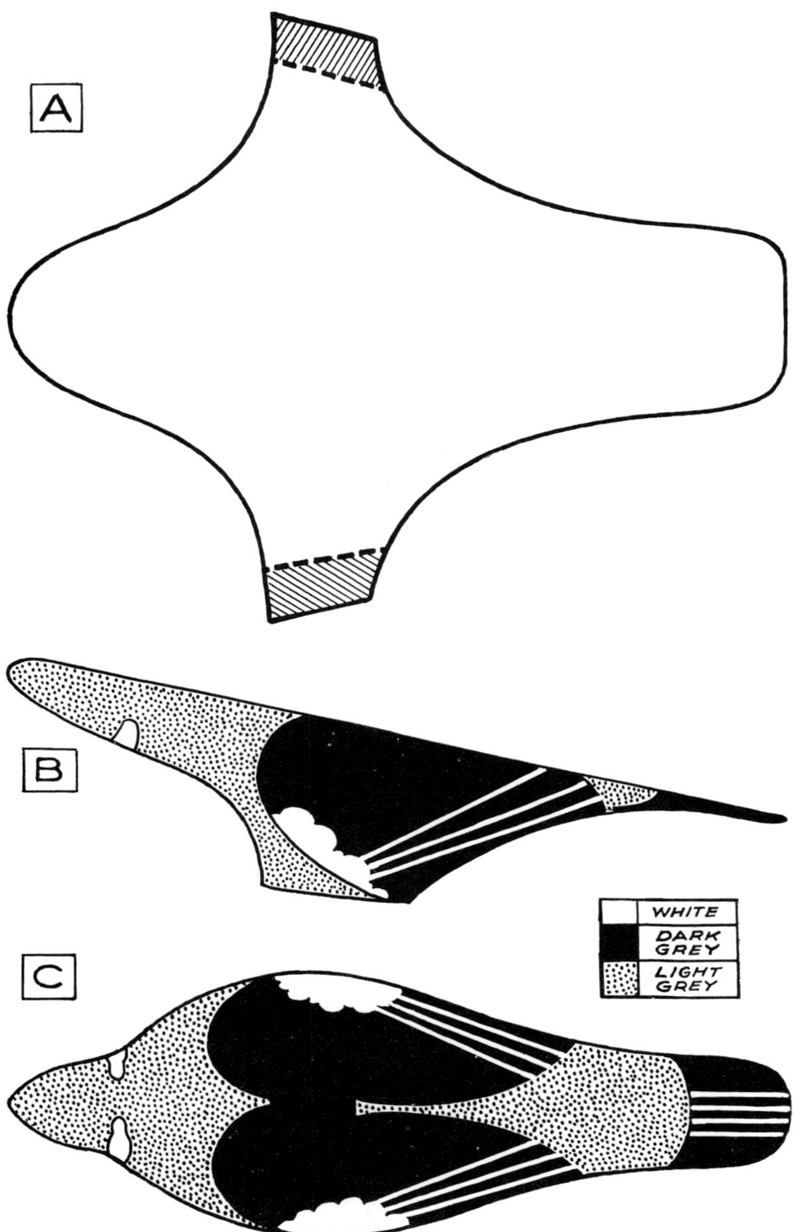


16. (A) Template; (B) side view; and (C) top view of home-made pigeon decoy.

lie one above the other. Using a waterproof glue, join the two flaps together, holding them in position with a couple of slip-on paper clips until they have set.

The decoy is now complete except for painting. It's as simple as that. Painting of *all* decoys, whether wooden carved replicas, or the Max Baker type, should be undertaken in the following manner.

First of all use a paint which will have a *matt* finish. Decoys which have a shiny look are absolutely useless in the field; with one exception, and that is when making stock-dove decoys, *the metallic green neck must shine*. It is difficult to purchase grey paint which will not shine, and the sportsman must, therefore, make his own matt finish. The various shades of grey are made by mixing black and white flat paints together until the required depth of colour is achieved. Pumice powder must be added to the paint mixture, in the ratio of about 1 oz. (28 g) pumice to each 8 oz. (230 g) of paint, in order to ensure a completely shine-free surface to the decoy.

One further hint: to ensure durability in the case of cardboard decoys, it is advantageous to cover the decoys with strips of ordinary cotton bandaging. This can be pressed down on to a well-glued surface and left to dry. The decoy takes on a more natural appearance in this way when painting is completed.

The general colouration of the various wild pigeons has been given at the end of Chapter 2, but for the guidance of the beginner, the pigeon should be painted (in the case of an adult wood-pigeon) as shown in Figs. 16B and 16C.

The completed decoy should appear as in Fig. 16B when viewed from the side.

For mounting these still decoys, a large paper clip, push-on type, should be bent in half: one half is fastened to a piece of dowelling and the overlapping flaps in the base of the bird are pushed into the free end.

An alternative method is to use a piece of galvanized wire the top of which is wound into a spiral. This is used in the same manner.

## *Moving Decoys*

These are made in a similar manner. The materials required are the same, except that the template is drawn in the pattern shown without, however, the side flaps. The mounting of the decoys will vary according to the ingenuity of the craftsman. The simplest method is that of mounting the decoy on to a piece of dowelling into the top of which a panel pin has been set, or to which a piece of wire has been bound. The pin pushed through a hole just *behind* the centre of balance of the decoy. The hole should be reinforced by two or three thicknesses of cardboard, or a small square of wood, glued to the underside of the bird. In this method of mounting the head of the decoy tilts towards the ground and each movement of the wind, when the decoys are placed head to wind, depresses the tail and causes the decoy to bob about in a lifelike manner. However, the decoy is apt to swing about out of the wind, perhaps even to point downwind, and may even blow off the pin with a sudden gust. The next method, therefore, is to mount two pins or two wire prongs on to the dowelling and insert these into two holes in the back of the decoy. One hole should be at the point of balance, the other an inch (25 mm) behind it. This prevents the decoys swinging about out of the wind.

This type of decoy may be utilized as a still decoy by fastening a piece of string across the bottom taking the place of the flaps on the first model.

None of these decoys is hard to make: the average person should be able to cut out and paint, with the first coat, at least twelve in an evening. Their cost is negligible – only a few pence or so each – and they will, with reasonable care, last several seasons. I made a nice 'field' of twenty-five decoys using cardboard which I obtained from old cartons, etc., and the only expense I had was in purchasing paint, of which I have a quantity left over for other decoys.

When painting these cardboard decoys it is as well to remember that they will often be placed in damp situations. It is essential therefore that the first coat of paint should cover both top and bottom of the decoy as well as the edges of the cardboard, in order to waterproof it.

In the case of the still decoys, if thin sheet metal is being used, the flaps which join the body of the bird together can be fastened with small nuts and bolts – Meccano nuts and bolts are very suitable – or they can be riveted together. The nut and bolt method is simpler and easier.

Sheet tin may be utilized, but should be allowed to rust before painting: simply immerse the completed decoys (prior to painting) in a bucket containing a vinegar-water solution, then hang outside overnight. The following morning they should have a beautiful rusty surface which takes the paint well and imparts a very natural, rough, finish.

Both the still decoys and the moving decoys may be fastened to lofting poles and raised to tree-top height if required.

*Another method of making decoys*

A very simple method of making decoys suitable for lofting and equally suitable for use on the ground, is that of stuffed fabric. These are constructed on the 'Rag Doll' principle. There is little or no skill required in their manufacture, and an elementary knowledge of the use of scissors and needle and thread is all that is necessary.

Lay a dead pigeon on its side on a piece of card. Arrange the bird in a natural position and then secure it by means of thread or thin cord taken over various parts of the bird's head, neck, body, and crossed *behind* the card itself. This binding or sewing to the card should be similar to the method used for mounting toy soldiers in their cardboard boxes.

When the bird has been properly fastened down take a soft lead pencil and trace its outline. Remove the bird from the card and you have a perfect template. Next, go round the marked silhouette with the pencil again but trace it half an inch (15 mm) larger all round. From this drawing excellent silhouette decoys may also be made.

For duck and other wildfowl decoys the template is then laid on to a sheet of cloth (any old clothing will do!) and the outline marked with tailor's chalk. The pattern marked is then cut out in duplicate. These sides are sewn together with the exception of a small opening in the underside, then turned inside out, stuffed with cellophane, wool sawdust, or kapok, and the opening sewn up. But for pigeons a further refinement is necessary. Ducks and waders are egg-shaped in appearance from above – pigeons widen out towards the tail. It is therefore necessary to mark out a further pattern to the shape of a triangle, thus representing a bird's tail when seen from above. The narrow portions of the pattern are joined at the head – the widest portion forms the trailing edge of the tail. If desired the beak can be omitted from the pattern. This makes for easier sewing, and in that event an ordinary golfing tee to represent the beak may be inserted and sewn up when the decoy has been stuffed. These decoys should be painted appropriately, and mounted on to a piece of wire.

If the craftsman prefers he can manufacture the simple cloth silhouette and then fix a piece of cardboard over the back of the bird to represent the tail. An alternative method is to make a wire frame to the right shape, cover it with material and add a couple of press studs to this 'tail' – it can then be fixed and removed quite simply for transportation purposes if a couple of press studs (or their counterparts) are sewn on to the back of the decoy.

*Movement and Decoys*

There are occasions when the sticks used to support decoys are not high enough. Examples of this occur when trying to decoy pigeons over tick-beans or sprouts. To set your field of decoys over such high growth in such a way that they can be seen by the pigeons would mean an inordinate number of high canes or stakes.

To cope with this situation I have evolved a method using a net base. This is stretched out over the decoy area and supported by at least four canes or stakes. Ordinary garden netting is suitable and easily obtained from general stores. A good size is 8 ft by 12 ft (2·4 x 3·6 m). That is easy to manage in a strong wind. The canes or stakes are first placed in position and then the netting stretched between them. It is not advisable to have the nets taut. A loose net on to which the decoys are placed is best because in any decent wind it moves and the decoys bob about. This movement is very attractive to hungry pigeons who will fly in to investigate.

17. Decoys set over cereals by means of a Netlon mesh base.

The normal full rubber decoy can be fastened into position on the netting by passing a rubber band over the head, under the net mesh, then up and over the tail. Any violent movement of the wind will not then toss the decoy overboard.

18. A net is stretched over the crop and supported by canes – the decoys may be laid on to the netting. In windy weather they may be secured to the nets by rubber bands.

Max Baker type of decoys can be fastened in a similar way, but the best method of securing them is to glue (by a modern adhesive such as Bostik or similar preparation) a short length of elastic to both sides of the decoy. An ordinary hook and eye, or press stud, is then sewn on to the other ends of the elastic and makes assembly and dismantling of the set-up quite easy.

To set the field on the nets, you must remember that each net only takes up about 50 to 90 square feet (5 to 8 sq m) and that three or more nets, placed some little distance apart are necessary. But, unlike normal decoying, you can place plenty of decoys on the nets. Birds feeding on sprouts will often form groups of six of more birds at one time on one sprout plant. So use plenty of decoys and don't forget to put decoys on the canes or supporting stakes as well.

Good sport can be assured by using these layouts over peas and beans.

Just as it is necessary to carry out a full reconnaissance of the shooting ground before commencing to set up a hide or to dig a pit, so it is essential to acquaint oneself with the area where decoys will be most successful. It is absolutely no use setting out decoys in a field where the pigeons know there is no feed: it is no use, for that matter, setting up decoys near a spot where the pigeons can expect much disturbance, e.g. near a footpath, by a gateway. Furthermore, for considerations of safety, the decoys must not be placed in such a position, in relation to the shooter, that the background is unsafe. Farm buildings in the direct line of fire at low birds, or a public right of way in the immediate background are obvious examples of dangeorus backgrounds.

The decoys should be placed about twenty to twenty-five yards (22·86 m) from the hide of the shooter and in this connection there are two schools of thought: the 'downwind' and the 'upwind'. In the former, the hide is placed downwind of the decoys: in the latter, the hide is placed upwind of the decoys. It is as well to remember that pigeon, in common with other birds, settle into the wind. If a hide is positioned downwind of the decoys, the shooting will be at birds coming in to the shooter, i.e. towards and over him. If the hide is placed upwind of the decoys the pigeon will not come in over the hide, but to one side of it, they should swing round and then come in to settle facing the hide. If placing a hide upwind of the decoys, it should be placed a little to one side as well. When using lofted decoys the best chance of making a big bag of pigeon is when shooting from downwind of the decoys.

The field, or lay-out, of the decoys requires careful consideration.

If the shooter follows the rule so often stated in articles in the sporting journals, and sets out his decoys head to wind, he is making a great mistake. I am afraid that this head-to-wind rule has become a sporting cliché and, though I expect a howl of protest from certain quarters, I must say that experience has taught me that it is not necessary. Study a field full of feeding pigeons: you will observe that the birds do not all face head to wind like grey-garbed ornithological guardsmen on parade. As they feed they turn from side to side, out of the wind. To achieve naturalness in setting out, therefore, one must vary the position of the birds a little: have some pointing to the left

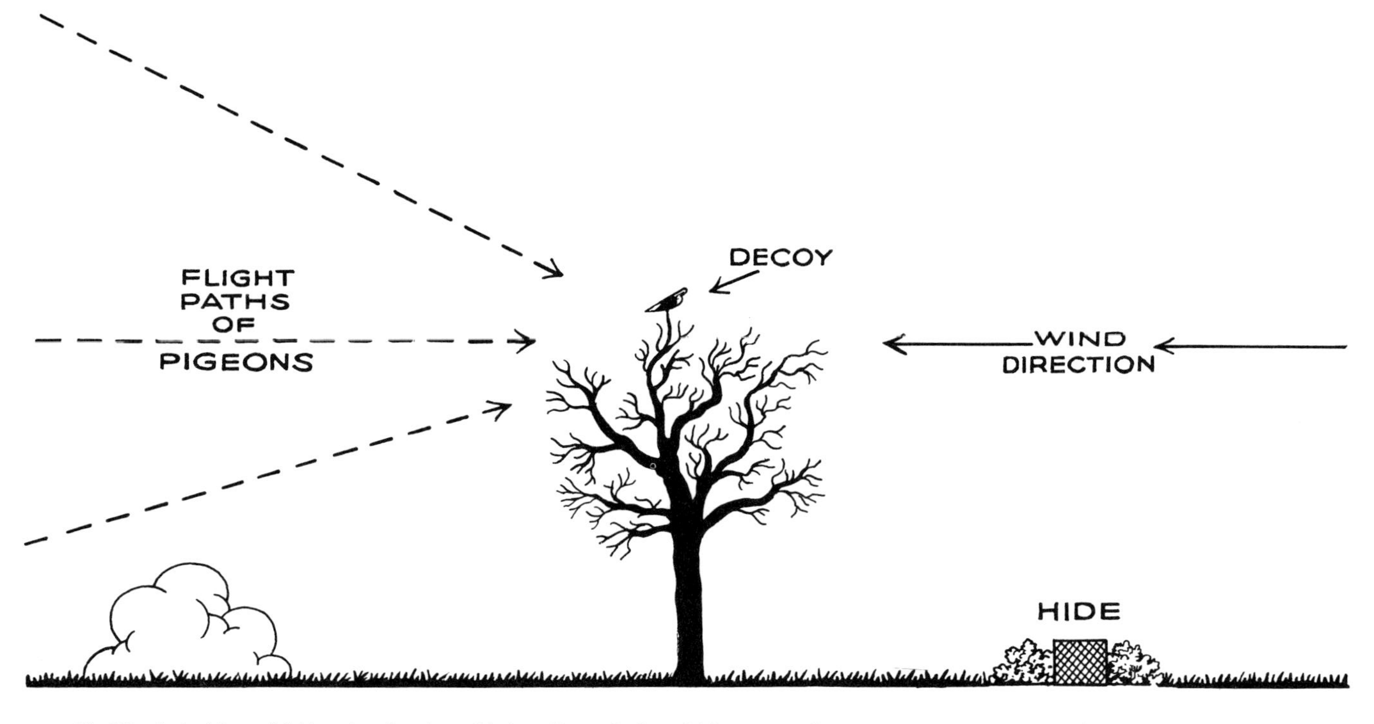


19. Upwind siting of hide, showing how birds will rarely be within range of shooter. For purposes of diagrams only one decoy, a lofted one, is shown.

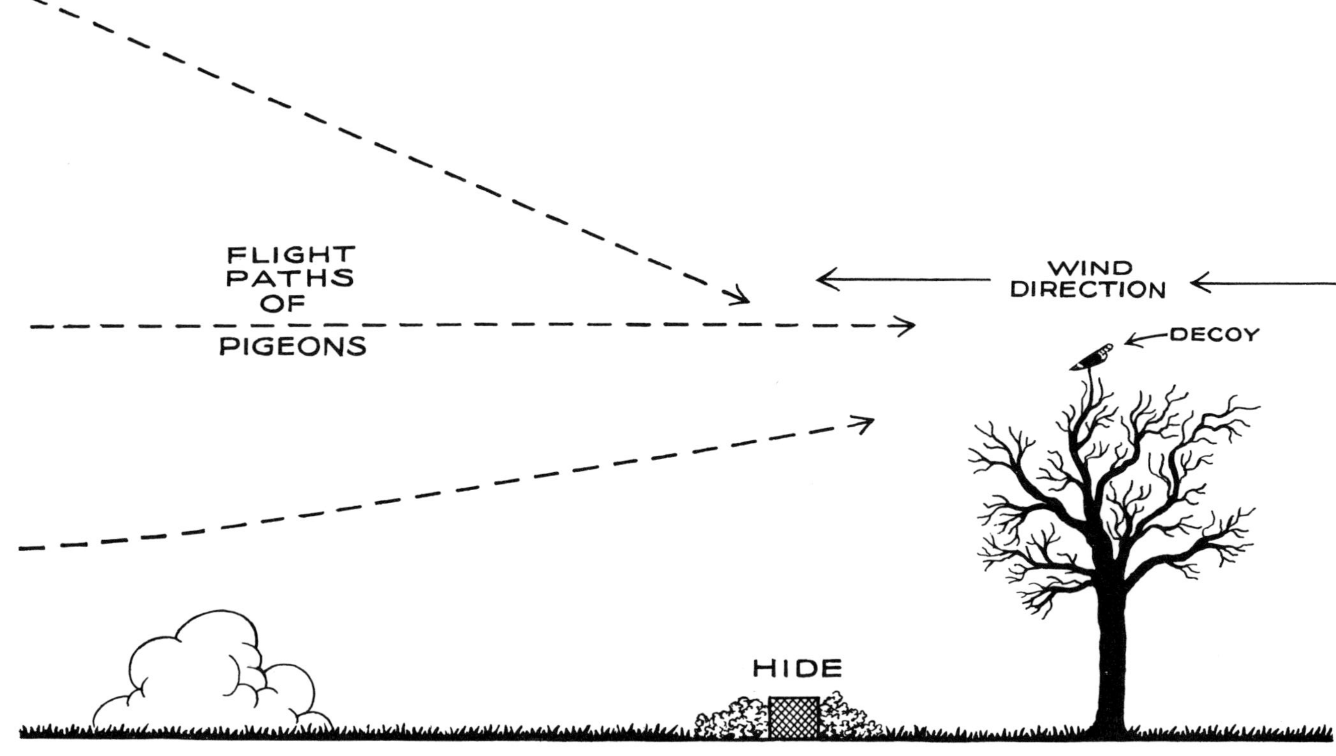


20. Downwind siting of hide, showing how birds will be within range of shooter.

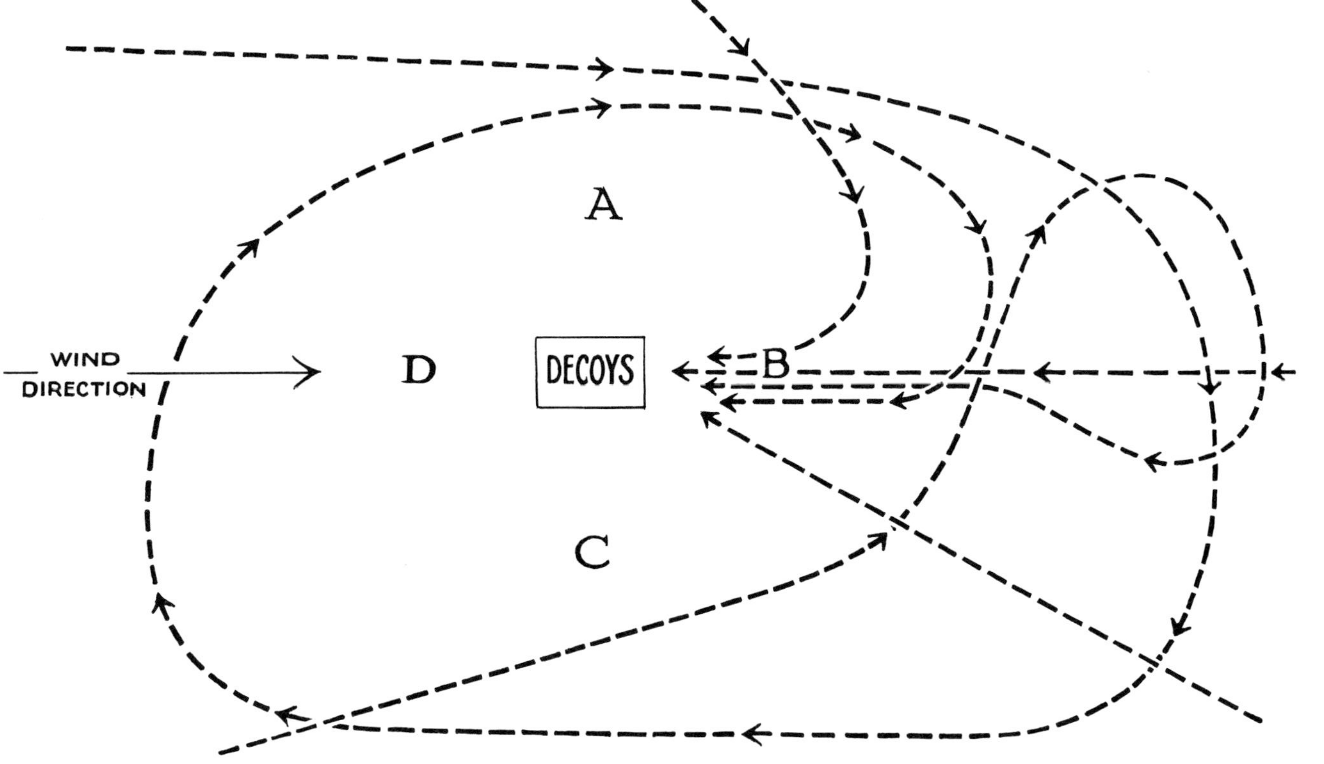


21. A diagram showing why the downwind siting of the hide is best when decoying. Note that the gunner at B, directly downwind, is sited directly on the flight paths of the pigeons (indicated by broken lines) no matter from what direction they approach the decoys.

and some to the right of the wind, and, of course, not all to the same degree. Remember also that the wind does not blow steadily from exactly the same quarter all the time, there are little variations in the direction and what at one minute could be a field of decoys head into wind could very well a few seconds later be a field of decoys all headed out of the wind! Do not, however, place any of the decoys at more than 90 degrees to the wind (and not as much as that if it is very strong) and certainly never place any of the decoys facing *downwind.* Of course, on windless days, or days when there is only a very slight air movement, the decoys should be placed facing in all directions.

It is also commonly stated that the decoys should be in front of the shooter. In general, this is not a bad rule, but the pigeon shooter should never go exactly by rule. A few decoys placed behind the shooter, a few to one side, and certainly one or more in the nearest high bush or tree improve the lay-out. If shooting from a pit or ditch, it is a very sound plan to place one or more decoys on the fence supports or posts about fifteen yards (14 m) from the hide. If shooting near the coast, or in an area where seagulls are common, the addition of a few decoy gulls, completes a very realistic picture and leads to the undoing of the pigeon, provided the sportsman is using 'straight' powder.

It is also a mistake to imagine that decoys should be placed on the pigeons' feeding grounds, or in the trees to which they will be fighting to roost, and nowhere else. I have enjoyed some really first-class pigeon shooting over lands which held no food for the pigeons, being simply rough pastures well frequented by the public, and without a roost for miles. In the centre of one of the pastures, which was a rather marshy place, with lots of rush beds, there was a shallow depression which always, no matter how lengthy a period of drought there might be, held a little water. To this depression – I can hardly call it a pond – the pigeons would come to drink, especially in the middle of the day. Now, as a rule pigeon shooting falls off in quality between about 9 a.m. and 2 p.m., but picks up again in the late afternoon so far as roost shooting is concerned. However, during the usual 'slack' period for other forms of shooting, I found that I could get first-rate sport with the pigeons at this drinking place. It was not even necessary to put any decoys out, and, no matter how hard I shot, nothing seemed to keep them away from the water when they were thirsty. This was most apparent after they had been feeding either on peas or corn, as post-mortem examinations of their crops revealed.

During the evening, too, before flighting to roost, the pigeons, during dry weather, would come to the water for a final drink.

22. A lofted decoy on a stick over a bush or hedge is often very effective.

Do not run away with the idea, however, that pigeon will come in to drink at any water-place. The side of the drinking hole must be shallow: a steeply banked pond is of no use whatever. Even so I recall such a pond, really a very small lake, which contained a shallow islet in the centre. The sides of the pond were at least 18 inches (about half a metre) in height but the little island had gently shelving sides, and to this the pigeons would flight in order to drink. The islet in the pond cancelled out the disadvantge of the steep banks and provided the scene of capital sport.

In addition to setting out the decoys, it is a wise plan, if the field is large, to put up some flags or pieces of rag or newspaper on sticks in order to (*a*) keep the birds in the air until they see the decoys and (*b*) 'drive' them or channel them towards your shooting position.

If there is a dead tree near the hide, and near the ground decoys, it is as well to place a lofted decoy high up in the bare branches. Pigeons like to use the naked arms of a dead tree as a lookout post, and often settle in one before dropping down to the decoys.

When setting out the recently shot birds, especially during the hot months, and especially if it is planned to take them home afterwards for the larder, they should be examined from time to time. Pigeons can become fly-blown remarkably quickly.

When leaving the shooting area at the end of the day, it is a good plan to scatter a little corn, or some peas about. This should be done, if possible, after the birds have gone to roost. The pigeons will soon find the feed and this will encourage them to stay in the vicinity where they are being shot, and at the same time do the farmer a good turn by keeping them away from his other crops, temporarily at any rate.

It is often said that loose feathers and/or dead birds should be removed from the scene as quickly as possible, because the presence of feathers or the sight of dead pigeons will scare the birds off. A little common sense is required in the interpretation of this rule. Certainly, if there is a lull in the shooting and provided one makes absolutely certain that no birds are approaching, it is a good idea to gather the dead birds as quickly as possible, and also to tidy up the loose feathers. I have to record, however, that I have had many good days with pigeons when the ground has been littered with feathers, and with birds. I have gathered the birds during the lulls in the shooting but never bothered to collect the plumage which covered the ground and on no single occasion did the sight of feathers scare the birds off.

If there is a wood, or a belt of trees, within a short distance of the shooting area, it is probable that birds are coming in to the decoys from that wood or trees. It might well be that, in spite of an apparent lull in the shooting and no birds visible, there are birds in those trees and to go out and tidy up the feather-strewn ground would be very noticeable to them.

Finally, do not expect to set out your decoys in the same spot day in and day out, time and time again. You cannot visit the same spot day after day and expect the pigeons to continue frequenting it. Though pigeons will stand hard shooting when coming in to drink, coming in to feed, or roosting, there is no bird more readily able to recognize a danger spot, no bird of a more timid disposition. If harrassed too frequently they will desert their customary grounds without hesitation.

Above all remember that the decoys must be seen by the birds and be at the same time easily visible to the shooter, who must, himself, remain invisible to the birds.

## CHAPTER 7

# Pigeon Shooting

Equipped with gun and cartridges, the knowledge how to construct a hide and where to place it, versed in the art of camouflage, and in possession of a set of decoys, the sportsman is now ready to engage the birds.

For the purpose of this chapter we may divide the shooting of pigeon into four classes:

(*a*) Shooting over decoys in the open.
(*b*) Shooting over decoys in covert.
(*c*) Flight shooting and roost shooting.
(*d*) Stalking (including rifle shooting).

### *Shooting over decoys in the open*

Having set out your decoys in the correct position, and constructed your hide or pit, wait for the first birds to come in. I will assume that you have started out for your shoot early enough to commence shooting about 8 a.m., or daylight if that is earlier. Keep yourself well hidden in the hide, do not bob up and down trying to spy out the land, sit and be patient. If you have set out a decoy in a nearby tree, it is possible that odd pigeons will fly in to inspect that decoy. Be ready to shoot them the moment they appear to be ready to settle, or as soon as possible thereafter; it is possible for the bird to take flight on noticing that the decoy is a strange, lifeless creature and swing off giving a difficult, if not impossible shot, on account of the intervening branches. That is one reason why I advocate shooting the bird just before it reaches the tree, as once it reaches it it is surprising how the twigs and branches will come between the bird and the shooter. If the bird settles, however, and the sportsman has a clear sight of it, shoot it sitting. For this purpose aim the barrel *at its feet*, otherwise you will probably shoot over it. Few men are able to aim a shotgun like a rifle and most shotguns are stocked to shoot a little high.

When the pigeons do begin to come in to the decoys wait until they are well within range. Keep absolutely still until the birds get within 25 yards (22·8 m) and then swing up the gun smoothly, quietly, without fluster and, still maintaining the swing, fire. It is sometimes advantageous to let the leading birds come in, or even settle, without shooting at them: this encourages larger numbers to follow suit.

Supposing that two birds come in, one behind another, and one settles. *Take the incoming bird first* when it is within range, because if you are using a double gun, you should be able to get the one that had settled immediately after killing the flying bird. It shouldn't have travelled very far by the time you swing on to it.

Sometimes it happens that the birds come in in flocks. A couple of barrels fired at them will probably cause them to depart somewhat hurriedly and if they do return, which is doubtful, it would be only after a long interval. Wave a piece of paper or handkerchief at them as they come in. This will divert the leading birds and split up the flock. The split-up flock will return again in smaller parties and give you prolonged shooting with better chances of success.

All the instructions about waiting for birds to get within 25 yards (22·8 m) not to shoot beyond 40 yards (36·5 m) and so forth, will probably be wasted on the beginner. Without experience he will probably be unable to judge the ranges accurately.

A simple method of learning to judge range is to take a dead bird and set it up, with wings closed, on the ground, and then step out the requisite number of yards (remember that paces, over rough ground, are not yards or metres, or anything like yards or metres) and try to remember what characteristics of the bird are easily apparent to the eye at the varying distances. Then set up the bird in a tree or on a fence post, and go through the whole procedure again. Finally, stretch out the wings of the bird, by placing wire under them, and set it up on a cane or stick about six or seven feet (1·8 or 2·1 m) high. Pace out the distances again at various angles from the bird, head on, going away, sideways, so that again you notice the various special characteristics of the plumage, silhouette, and so forth, which will enable you to judge shooting distances accurately and quickly.

During frosty weather, or when the contryside lies under a mantle of snow, the white background makes the birds seem much closer than they are in reality: the same optical illusion occurs in foggy conditions.

There is no need to go out into the shooting field to learn distance and range judging. In most of the large towns there are flocks of town pigeons which feed in the streets and public squares, or in the municipal parks and gardens. The observant sportsman can avail himself of these opportunities to watch the birds, study their habits, and estimate his distance from them. A rather amusing incident, amusing to the passer-by at any rate, occurred in the busy streets of the City when a friend and I, watching the pigeons wheeling over Smithfield Market, judged which birds were in range and which were not. We raised imaginary guns and shot (or missed!) the birds as they flew round. Five minutes of practice like this are very useful, but we were very nearly accused of busking by a suspicious member of the City Police!

Occasionally pigeons will drop in beyond the decoys, sometimes they will settle amongst them, and the dummies do not seem to scare them. A friend of mine, on a pigeon shooting occasion over a Lincolnshire pea field, set up a dead bird as a decoy. Within a few moments a cock bird flew in, circled, then settled beyond the set-up bird. Bowing and blowing he circled the decoy, and then tried to tread it. This was too much for Geoffrey who immediately shot it. This is not an unusual occurrence; amorous pigeons have been known to try and tread even wooden or rubber decoys. Sometimes other birds will figure in the bag. I have known sparrow-hawks strike at decoy birds, and on one occasion even had a kestrel strike at one of my Max Bakers. I have never heard of this species behaving in this way before. It may have been an isolated instance; on the other hand it may well be that young pigeons do figure on the kestrel's menu. The amazing thing about it was that the kestrel circled the field of decoys twice before he dropped on to them, so it was no mere accident.

For this form of shooting a ·410 shotgun is excellent, provided the gunner is not a novice. The small report does not disturb birds directly to windward as a 12-bore would.

Most of the shooting literature informs the enthusiast that decoy shooting is not possible when the ground is covered with snow, but under these conditions decoying is possible over greens, and even on the open fields. If shooting the open fields it is essential to sweep a quantity of snow away from the ground within twenty or thirty yards (18·3 to 27·4 m) of the ambush. After sweeping this patch clear, throw a little feed into it, wait for a day or so, then, on the shooting morn set the decoys out on this patch. Good bags are often made this way.

Windy weather, the wilder the better, is best for good pigeon shooting. The birds, in these conditions, fly lower and feed nearer the shelter of trees and fences.

Sometimes the sportsman will have birds coming in towards him: he will follow out the old shooting rule and 'blot them out' with his barrels in the approved manner just before he fires. What should have been a successful shot often results, in these circumstances, in a clean miss. The birds are, more often than not, losing height, albeit imperceptibly, and by swinging ahead, or blotting out the bird with the barrel (the correct thing to do with straight incoming birds) he is actually shooting over them. To achieve success, swing with the bird and pull the barrel down slightly so that the bird appears *over* the barrels, like a going away bird, at the moment of firing.

If the bird is hit and a cloud of feathers descends from it, watch that bird carefully. It may fly a considerable distance before dropping dead: it may even travel to a wood, or tree, there to settle, and there to die. If the bird flies on, apparently strongly, inspect the loose feathers as soon as convenient without interfering with the shooting. Nine times out of ten the gunner will find that these feathers are small white, down feathers from the hinder parts and legs of the bird. These indicate that he was shooting too far behind, that in reality the bird has been missed, struck only by stray marginal or fringe pellets from the pattern. If these down feathers are the only evidence of a hit, rest assured that the bird has not been wounded, mortally or otherwise.

The sportsman will have to use his discretion about gathering birds at the end of a day. If birds have fallen into standing corn, for example, you would probably do more harm to the farmer than the birds do, if you go in and trample his crops about looking for a dropped bird. Count birds falling in standing corn as lost. I have had to count several such losses in my shooting life and though I don't like leaving ungathered birds, there is the consoling thought in these circumstances that the operation was one of vermin control, where killing is more important than gathering.

### *Shooting over decoys in covert*

This is a very successful method of shooting pigeons. The first essential, for a good day's sport, is a strong wind, and like the shore-shooter the pigeon shooter should pray for a *gale*.

This form of shooting need not commence so early in the morning as its counterpart over the fields, and, unlike open decoy work, there is often fairly continuous shooting throughout the day. The reason for this is that in the early morning the birds fly out of covert to the fields to feed, but during the daytime they make frequent excursions back to the covert.

Place your hide as near to the outside of the wood as you are able. If there are a few bushes or small trees, or other cover, beyond the wood (say twenty to forty yards (18·3 to 36·5 m) it is as well to site the hide there. Place the decoys in the high trees behind you, and position your hide downwind of the decoys. The pigeons will fly directly towards the decoys giving you reasonable shots, and, if flying into a strong wind their ground speed will be comparatively slow, thereby affording easier shots. Do not fire at the birds, which will streak downwind whether overhead or to one side of you: they will presently return at a lower height and at a much slower speed.

If the undergrowth is very thick it may be very difficult to find dropped birds. Though dogs can be a disadvantage when shooting from a hide over open fields (unless one has got a really decent sized shooting pit), in the woods it is a different matter and under these conditions a dog is essential to get the fullest enjoyment out of the sport. Some dogs are apt to be shy of retrieving pigeons – the loose feathers seem to discourage them – but with care and patience this can be overcome.

If using a dog, remember to provide some overhead cover for it. You cannot expect a keen animal to stay absolutely motionless for hours on end and overhead cover will prevent the birds seeing either the dog or any movements it may make.

When shooting birds in covert you must place your decoys about a foot *clear of the top of a tree*. If they are placed in the lower branches, or in the side of a tree, they are not visible to birds coming from the opposite side. Kept well aloft they are visible from all quarters and form a deadly attraction. Watch carefully to see that the effects of the strong wind, causing the trees to sway, do not swing your decoys out of the correct position, causing them to slip, or slide into an unnatural position. Nothing scares a bird off more quickly than an unnatural position.

For this form of shooting it is a good idea to have two or three hides ready for occupation so that you may change position to suit the varying circumstances. A typical change, of course, is the position of the sun in relation to the shooter. The sun may be on his right side when he commences shooting, but during the middle of the day he may find himself shooting into it. There is nothing more exasperating than trying to shoot into the sun. The gun is swung up on to an easy bird and then, right at the very moment of firing, the bird disappears into the blinding light of old Sol; result, a clean miss. Always try to place yourself so that the sun is to one side or behind you: with the sun behind you the birds are at a disadvantage. Fighter-pilots are trained to come in to the enemy from 'out of the sun'.

### *Flight and roost shooting*

There is great similarity between these two methods of shooting.

There may be occasions when the only way the sportsman can obtain pigeon shooting is to intercept the birds on their way from roosts to feeding grounds, neither of which may be on the land he has permission to shoot over. Under such conditions he must take a leaf out of the wildfowler's books and indulge in what we call 'flighting' and our American cousins call 'pass shooting'.

The first essential is to ascertain the route the birds are accustomed to take. This will vary according to the weather conditions and the direction of the wind. Birds which cross land from a certain direction in a south-east wind, for example, may miss that land altogether if the wind blows from the west, or may come in from an altogether different quarter. Strong winds mean that the birds fly lower and seek the shelter of hedges more closely. This slowing up of flight, of course, only applies if the birds are flying into the wind: it may well be that the direction of the wind is such that the birds fly with it, and that may increase their speed enormously. This makes for difficult, if spectacular, shooting – though, personally, I always prefer to take a fast down wind shot at a bird than the easier head-on shots. Success in such conditions means that the bird killed is remembered when the larger bags of easier days are forgotten. Pride in the execution of the job is a good thing in shooting because it breeds confidence, and confidence in oneself and in the gun, as well as in the ammunition, is half the battle in straight shooting.

Having ascertained the routes taken by the birds, the shooter should then look for suitable positions from which he can intercept them. It is not necessary to have a hide prepared – a portable hide is sufficient. The shelter of a hedge, bush or wall, over which the birds will fly is good enough, provided that the shooter keeps still and remains hidden until the moment of firing. With properly camouflaged clothing and the minimum of movement, it is possible to sit or stand *in front of* a hedge or other cover and take the birds there and then. Standing or sitting in front of a natural background is actually better than shooting from a hide, because you are able to keep the birds under observation all the time.

Flight shooting *may*, and I say 'may' deliberately, mean that the sportsman requires a longer chambered gun than the normal game gun. A wildfowl gun may be necessary because of the height at which the birds will fly, but a bird 120 feet (36·5 m) up seems much farther away than he really is. If the sportsman wishes to engage pigeons at greater distances, I would strongly advocate the use of 'low velocity' loads, up to $1\frac{1}{4}$ oz. (35·4 g) of shot, with a reduced powder charge, fired from his normal game gun. Such cartridges will be loaded on request at one's gunsmith: alternatively cartridges on the market, shooting $1\frac{1}{16}$ oz. (33·7 g) of shot, giving normal game gun breech pressures, are excellent. The extra pellets mean that you can use a heavier-sized pellet if you wish, keeping the same or nearly the same pattern density, or increase your pattern density with your normal-sized shot.

In this form of shooting, of course, no decoys are necessary – nor would they be of any use.

To give an idea of the use of flight shooting. I had a shoot within half-an-hour of the Bank of England, where I found excellent pigeon shooting. Near by is a sort of parkland or common, used by the public, and to which a few local gunners repair in search of sport. The pigeons fly over that ground to reach my small roost, and other fields in the area where they feed. One day, sitting with my back to a boundary hedge, shooting over decoys, I was amazed to see my birds which should have come confidently, streak past me in panic. A few seconds later I heard the double report of a shotgun. The day passed and I enjoyed only a little sport compared with my usual shooting. At the end of the afternoon I was about to take a bird coming in to my decoys when I heard a gun fired from the other side of my hide. Outraged I stood up and got ready to deliver a tirade of words at the offender. A cheerful grin in the face of a humorous-looking man met me: a pair of laughing eyes peering through the fence met my angry ones. Before I could say anything the intruder spoke. 'Say you 'coys are okay,' he said. 'Noticed you bin usin' them some weeks now, and you've bin bringing all the birds in over the Chase.'

I realized what he was driving at but words were beyond me.

' 'Ad some sport,' he confided. 'Regular flight line of them to your birds. Got a couple this arternoon. Hope you don't mind?!'

I draw a veil over what I said, but ultimately we joined forces and sank a couple of tankards of ale in the nearest hostelry.

That man, limited for shooting to a public common (whether he had a right to do so or not I never tried to ascertain since it was none of my business anyway), had been observant enough to note that there was a regular flight line of birds over the common to my decoys. He took advantage of it, and, like the wildfowler he happened to be, stationed himself in such a position that he was able to intercept the flighting pigeon. That his tactics militated against my sport was merely incidental and I certainly bear him no ill will for it. On the contrary I had to admire his intelligent appreciation of the conditions, and keen observations of the pigeons' habits.

Flight shooting at pigeons is, however, a chancy business. There are more blank days than successful days, but often it is the only sport available. Full and accurate observation of the ground and the routes the birds take are the keystones on which successful flight shooting is founded.

The sportsman, who likes to maintain a good average of kills per cartridges expended, will soon find that pigeon shooting, apart from days over the decoys, will soon deflate his ego in that respect. I know of no other wild bird, even including wildfowl, which can so easily ruin the good run of kills a shooter has been maintaining. Roost shooting often results in more shots being fired than pigeons collected, but pigeon flighting is more difficult. Do not despair, therefore, if on some occasions you expend a whole box of cartridges for four or five pigeons gathered: even well-known sportsman have been known to fare far worse at this branch of the sport. On the other hand, there is a certain amount of satisfaction in pulling off tricky shots at fast birds, which more than compensates the shooter for his misses. Flighting pigeon has a charm of its own and is, unfortunately, all too often neglected.

Whereas flight shooting may extend over the whole of the day – roost shooting is limited to a brief period only. Nevertheless this short period is often crammed with excitement, and as many shots, or even more, may be fired in this short time as during an entire day of flighting.

Pigeons go to roost early. In January the best chance of sport is from 2.30 to 4.30: in February, about half an hour later: in March the period is from abut 4.30 to 5.30. November roughly corresponds to February, while December shooting times at the roost approximate to those in January. It must be remembered, however, that if the day darkens early through meteorological conditions – mist, or heavy banks of clouds – the birds will come to roost earlier. They will also fly in earlier in very windy weather.

Roost shooting is least successful on clear, windless days. On those occasions the pigeons will come in very high, so that they appear as small as starlings. They will circle the woods at a considerable height before suddenly plunging down to settle in the trees. This sudden descent of the birds has caused more barrels to be discharged with no result whatever than any other action by the birds. It is, unfortunately a habit for the average sportsman in such circumstances to fire at the birds when they are still too high. The sudden descent from an out of range altitude is apt to fluster most shots and if the gun is not discharged when the birds are still out of range. they are often fired when the bird is in range but no lead given. In other words the sportsman forgets to drop his barrel ahead of the birds with the result that the shot flies high behind them. It is not an easy trick to master, this pulling down of the barrels, especially as the sportsman has to put the gun up first to get on to his bird. There are two or three methods of overcoming this fault. One is to bring the gun up to one side of the bird, smoothly and evenly, without the sudden movements which scare the bird off: then bring the gun round in an arc behind the bird, down in front of him and slightly increase the speed of the swing as you pass his head and still maintaining the swing squeeze the trigger: do not stop the barrel movement on squeezing the trigger or you will shoot behind. Follow through the swing as a golfer follows through with his club striking (or missing!) the ball. What really happens is that you aim on to the bird, slightly pause, calculate his speed when swinging with him, and then (though you may not be aware of it) anticipate the amount of lead to give him by increasing the speed of your swing. The whole movement should be done in one harmoniously executed act.

Another method is to bring the gun up to the bird and then commence to pull the barrel down with the left hand until you see at least a foot of daylight between the bird and muzzle: maintaining this gap by still swinging, squeeze the trigger and the bird should be yours.

If you are standing in a spot quite close, within a few paces only, of the tree into which the bird is dropping, it is as well to wait until that split second when he drops his tail (which acts as an air-brake) before settling. At that moment he presents a comparatively easy target – he is almost sitting in the air, as it were – and, by aiming the shotgun in the manner of a rifle at his feet, you should get good results.

When taking up position for roost shooting you should place yourself on the sheltered side of the wood. This may not be possible, of course, as lands over which you have no permission to shoot may march up to the wood boundary. The birds always prefer the sheltered side and wherever possible, in this form of shooting, stand with your back to the wind.

Roost shooting is often undertaken without decoys. This is a great pity because decoys add to the attractiveness of the sport and enhance the possibilities of getting good bags. If you stand downwind of lofted decoys, which have been placed high as possible, no matter how the pigeon wheel about before coming in, they will invariably fly in to the decoys against the breeze and should pass over your head, or within reasonable range on either side.

Although I have given a rough estimate of the time at which roost shooting commences, it is always as well to get into position a little earlier so that no disturbance will be made if the pigeons should come in unexpectedly. It is often a good plan to get well downwind of the roost, when the weather is boisterous. First of all, however, set out your decoys and then get under cover of some hedge, or in a hide, two or three hundred yards (185 or 275 m) from the wood. During such weather conditions pigeon often collect some considerable distance away and flight in to roost in a long, continuous stream. Quite often they will play follow-my-leader through a gap in trees, and then they afford excellent shooting. When dusk approaches the shooter can vacate his flight spot and take up position within range of his decoys. In calm weather, however, this practice is useless and then it is advisable for the sportsman to take up his position on the edge of the wood, for the birds will come in from all directions and not in the long streams which rough weather brings.

When you have taken up position for roost shooting *allow the first few birds to come in unharmed.* If you shoot at these leaders you will, in all probability, drive them away to other woods and your sport will be abruptly curtailed. Again, do not shoot at high birds, you will only frighten them away. I have been to several organized roost shoots and I have seen more chances wasted through shooting at out of range birds, and early birds, than one would credit. I know that it is the policy of many organized shoots, spread over a wide area, to 'keep the birds on the move'. This may drive them to another district, but it achieves nothing and may even be harmful because (1) the birds seek other quarters where they can carry on their raids to the detriment of the farmers and (2) much powder and shot is wasted which otherwise could be put to good use.

I recall typical evenings when, in position and ready for the birds to come in, I have seen the pigeons circling the woods, or speeding in like arrows at a great height. If given a peaceful interlude they will drop in and afford easy shots. Yet sooner or later some 'clot' (to coin a modern, but very expressive term, though at the time one thinks of stronger, duel-provoking adjectives) has to let go with one or both barrels at such birds, spoiling the sport not only for himself, but for others also. At the end of the evening this typical sportsman, as often as not an experienced game shot, will remark: 'By gad, fired thirty shots for one bird. I'm sure I dropped eight or nine, I saw the feathers fly, but they carry a lot of shot.'

Let us be honest: the one bird that sportsman bagged was a fluke. As for the feathers: they were figments of the imagination while the eight or nine he was sure he 'dropped' were children of a fertile brain trying to bolster up its ego, afraid to admit to no score, trying to excuse itself and also to impress others.

By waiting for the chances which should come – if they do not it will not make any difference to the bag anyway, while some expensive cartridges will have been saved – the shooter should be able to take his birds with fair certainty of success. The object of pigeon shooting is twofold, to provide sport, and to cut down the numbers of an agricultural menace. I am sure that it is better for a party of even a dozen shots at such a 'battue' to fire only four or five cartridges in the aggregate, and to collect three or four birds, than to fire over a hundred cartridges, for a couple of dozen or so birds.

Good roost shooting may be enjoyed when several parties are out over adjoining farms or estates. The birds are then 'kept on the move' in the approved manner, but in these circumstances it is just as well to

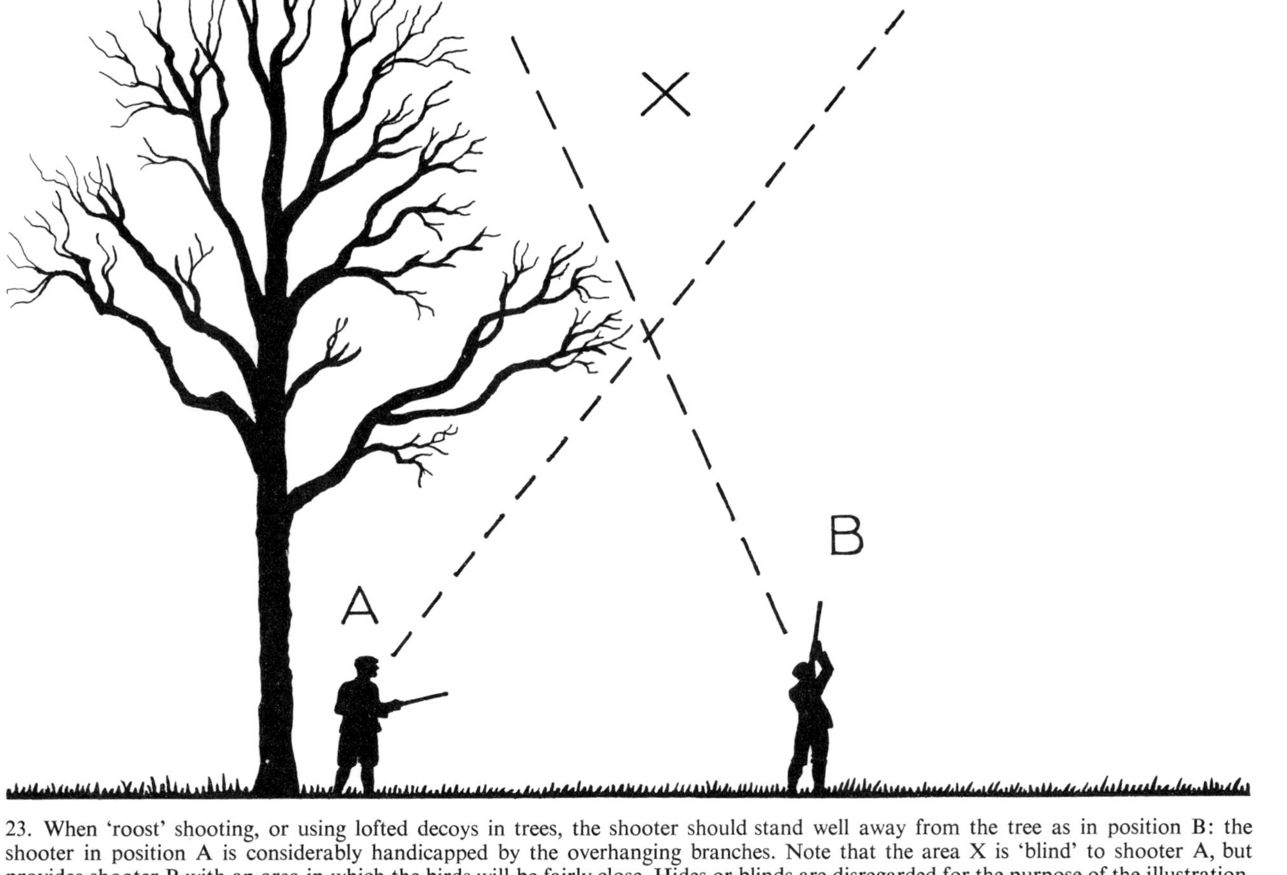


23. When 'roost' shooting, or using lofted decoys in trees, the shooter should stand well away from the tree as in position B: the shooter in position A is considerably handicapped by the overhanging branches. Note that the area X is 'blind' to shooter A, but provides shooter B with an area in which the birds will be fairly close. Hides or blinds are disregarded for the purpose of the illustration.

allow early arrivals to find a little sanctuary and concentrate on the late, tired arrivals.

The edge of the wood, if it is extensive is, not always the best position. Sometimes the sportsman may find a clearing with a high, dead tree in it, surrounded by conifers. Should he have a sufficient space between the tree tops to give him a good, open shooting background, such a position can give excellent sport. I have known occasions when the edges of the woods have been surrounded by sportsmen waiting for the birds to come in. I have used decoys and stood in such a clearing. Despite the wild shooting of the outer-circle the birds have come in to me! What happens is that they circle the wood at a great height, then drop right into the centre of it, out of range, very often out of sight, of the circle of anxious sportsmen ringing the trees. By waiting, by not being impatient at hearing the heavy firing from the different positions around me, by not being discouraged at seeing no birds appearing, I have, in due course, been rewarded by the sight of pigeon plummeting in towards my decoys. I have waited to let the first birds settle – and it is surprising how they will settle in spite of the barrage going on around them – and then taken the following birds which often come in singly: In this manner, though I have sometimes only had half a dozen shots, I have often returned with nearly as many birds (sometimes as many) as cartridges expended. Sick birds – that is those which have been struck, but not mortally wounded – often make for the centres of such clearings. They afford easier shots and, though to some minds it might savour of poaching, it is not, because you are performing an act of good sportsmanship in terminating the sufferings of the bird, and you are not deliberately bagging another man's quarry. Of course, if you hear a shot from one of your companions and immediately thereafter see a hit bird making for you, it is your duty to kill it and return it to him. But do not, for heaven's sake, announce that you 'finished it off'. Let him think that you retrieved a dead bird for him. That is common sense and plain courtesy.

Sometimes it is advantageous to stand in a ride. Get slightly in front of one line of trees, so that their branches do not obstruct your overhead shots. If the pigeons come in over the other side you should stand a very fair chance of pretty shooting as they top the trees ahead of you. This method has the advantage that the range is known beforehand, and the height of the birds easily calculated.

Above all, try to pull down your birds *before* they reach your decoys as up to that moment there is less chance of that elusive swerve which nine times out of ten results in $1\frac{1}{16}$ oz. (30·1 g) of expensive lead thrown into the air behind or below them.

*Stalking and rifle shooting*

Good fun may be had in stalking birds either on their feeding grounds, or whilst they are sitting in the trees. In the former case the use of all available cover, hedges, dykes, ditches, walls must be made use of. It is possible to get in, at most, two shots in this manner. One on the ground and one in the air. Remember that the closed wings and full crops of the bird help to protect it and slightly larger pellet sizes may be necessary, perhaps 5's. When stalking pigeon in the woods, the best weather is fog at daybreak, because then the birds have a tendency to sit tight and refuse to leave the shelter of the trees. Though they are not unduly sensitive of hearing, nevertheless they have exceedingly keen eyesight and it needs careful Red Indian tactics to get within shot of them. This task is almost impossible when the trees are full of leaf. But remember when stalking in the winter months, when the trees are devoid of foliage, that while it is easier for you to spot the birds, it is doubly so for them to see you.

Pigeons have an uncanny knack of placing the branches of a tree between themselves and the gunner. But, invariably, when taking off from a tree they start with a loud clap of wings and a sudden downward swoop. The bottom of this downward swoop is the time and place to take them, otherwise they climb rapidly and the tendency is to shoot below them.

Richard Jefferies in *The Gamekeeper at Home* describes a method of wood-pigeon shooting which I have never come across though I have often thought it might be worth while. He describes pigeon shooting *by moonlight*.

'Many pigeons roost in the oaks of the hedges,' he says, 'choosing by preference one well hung with ivy, and when it is a moonlit night afford tolerable sport. It requires a gun on each side of the hedge. A stick flung up awakes the birds; they rise with a rush and clatter, and in the wildness of their flight and the dim light are difficult to hit. There is a belief that pigeons are partially deaf. If stalked in the daytime they take little heed of footsteps or slight noises which would alarm other creatures; but on the other hand, they are quick of eye, and are gone directly anything suspicious appears in sight. You may get quite under them and shoot them on the bough at night. It is not their greater wakefulness, but the noise they make in rising which renders them good protectors of preserves; it alarms other birds and can be heard at some distance.'

A word of warning may be necessary here. Sportsmen who are not wildfowlers may be tempted, in light of this passage, to try out this method. I have had some considerable fowling experience and, though Jefferies does not mention it in this passage, it is essential that the moon be lightly veiled by cloud, so that the whole sky forms a lovely, white, translucent curtain. Against this 'backcloth' the birds will be seen fairly easily, and if seen they are in range, not only of a 12-bore, but of smaller calibre guns. For example, under such a moonlit sky I have shot widgeon on the mudflats with a ·410 adaptor in a 12-bore shotgun. If the moon is full and clear, then it would be useless for the purpose of shooting pigeon, or any other birds, because the background of sky would be black and the birds would not be seen at all.

There is also the question of the gathering of shot birds to be considered. In wildfowling this is often difficult enough, even though the birds drop on to mud which may shine like silver. Consider the difficulties attendant upon trying to find a bird dropped into thick cover. However, it does sound an attractive way of shooting pigeons, even though I should imagine that not more than a couple of shots would be fired of an evening.

Stalking is, of course, at its best when practised with a miniature rifle. And, when I use the term miniature rifle I include not only small calibre firearms, but also the modern air-rifle.

As I have suggested earlier in this book. I would recommend a target rifle for field shooting at pigeons. My reasons are two-fold; firstly the rifle is much more accurate and secondly its increased weight makes for a better firing platform. I am not decrying the modern sporting model miniature rifle, but the head of a pigeon is a very small target and there is no excuse at all for a decent rifle shot to hit the birds anywhere else. I have read in sporting journals about pigeon travelling half a mile with a ·22 bullet in the body. The man who wrote that should be ashamed of himself. Aimed at the head the result would be either a clean kill or a clean miss. There should be no body shots deliberately aimed or otherwise. The reason why the birds are sometimes hit in the body is solely because the rifleman is at too great a distance to hit the head with accuracy. The continual movements of the bird make difficult shooting in so far as the head target is concerned and the lazy, or incompetent, sportsman aligns his sights on the larger area of the pigeon's body.

It is not easy to hit a bird high up in the branches of trees which are in continual movement due to the wind. The golden rule, therefore, is to shorten your rifle work to not more range than sixty yards (54·8 m), and even this is a long way for accurate pigeon shooting. The idea of using rifle a at 100 yards (91·5 m) on wood-pigeon is fantastic unless a telescope sight is used. Personally I would prefer to limit the range to approximate shotgun range! This may sound like heresy, but the true sportsman aims to kill cleanly, and the longer ranges render clean kills less certain unless the rifleman is in the 'expert' category.

For pigeon shooting the short ·22 bullet is ample. The high velocity ammunition causes a sound-barrier crack which can be very disturbing to the birds, and the sound, made by the passage of the bullet through the air in its flight, cannot be dampened down by a sound moderator or silencer. Using the short ·22 cartridge, the muzzle report can be eliminated by a sound moderator, while the comparatively slow flight of the projectile does not scare the birds. With a telescope sight shooting becomes easier, and more difficult at the same time. It becomes easier to miss because the mistakes the sportsman makes are magnified by the telescope; consequently what might well be a miss by one inch (25 mm) over open iron sights, may be as much as four inches (101 mm), or more when using the telescope sights. On the other hand kills are much cleaner.

Great care should be exercised when using a rifle for pigeon shooting. It must be remembered that the background must be safe. Particularly is great care required in shooting pigeons *over decoys with a rifle*. I have seen some very pretty shooting by one sportsman who used to knock down the birds at the moment they hung in the air before settling – but he was well down in a pit when he shot, so that his bullets were aimed into the sky, Furthermore the background was open sea.

If using a ·22 rifle for pigeon shooting, it is as well to make certain that your Firearms Certificate does not limit the use of your weapon to approved ranges. If it does, take steps to get it amended, otherwise you will be using your weapon in an 'unauthorized manner' and might thereby incur the pains and penalties prescribed by the Firearms Act, 1937 – not the least of which might be withdrawal of your permit and a refusal to grant you another one.

The ballistics enthusiast may be interested in the comparison between a ·22 Long Rifle, High Velocity cartridge and the ·22 Short Standard cartridge I recommend. The weight of the bullet in the former (am here referring to I.C.I. ammunition) is 40 grains (2·6 g); the bullet weight of the latter, 30 grains (1·9 g). At the muzzle, the energy in foot-pounds of the former is 174, of the latter a mere 57. At fifty yards (45·7 m) the energy in foot-pounds drops, in the case of the L.R.H.V. ammunition, to 121, and in the Short ammunition to 46. In either case it is much more than sufficient to kill a pigeon. As for trajectory, the drop of the L.H.R.V. ammunition at fifty yards (45·7 m) is 2·5 inches (65 mm), whereas the Short ammunition is 5·5 inches (139 mm). There is, therefore, a little more latitude in sighting so far as the Long Rifle, High Velocity cartridge is concerned, but that is its sole advantage, for pigeon shooting.

If you hold a Firearms Certificate and wish to fit, or have fitted, a sound moderator, it will be necessary to apply to the police to have the Certificate altered to enable you to acquire such an accessory.

When stalking pigeon with the rifle there will inevitably be some 'off-hand' shooting from a standing or kneeling position. This is not easy without considerable practice. One good tip is to practise this form of shooting on small pieces of wood, approximately the size of a pigeon's head. Comparatively few riflemen are able to take an absolutely steady aim when standing, and the sporting rifleman (as opposed to the target man) must practise creeping and walking towards his target, and then taking aim and squeezing the trigger the moment the sights are 'on'. There must be no delaying, holding, or hanging on.

From the ·22 rifle we come, naturally, to the air-rifle available in both ·177 and ·22 calibre. For sporting shooting the ·22 pellet is preferable on the grounds that it is double the weight of the ·177 pellet. The chief advantage of the air-rifle is that it is soundless in action. I have used air-rifles against furred and feathered vermin, including cormorants, at up to seventy yards (64 m) and when I have missed I have been able to re-cock, load and fire again, scoring a clean kill with the next, or even third shot. In the absence of report, the flying pellets do not disturb the targets. Do not purchase an air-rifle which is cocked by means of a 'break-down' action: see that the barrel and air-chamber are in one piece. Otherwise you will find that with continual use there will develop an air leak at the junction of breech face and air cylinder, in addition to which there will be a tendency for the barrel to drop downwards, which interferes with the sighting. Air-rifles are heavier than most sporting model miniature firearms, and approximate more the weight of target rifles, generally being in the region of 8 lb. (3·6 kg), as opposed to the normal 5¼ lb. to 6 lb. (2·4 to 2·7 kg) of the sporting rifle.

Sport with the rifle is at its best when the days are calm, when there is no wind to toss the branches about. It is possible to sit in a hide within a dense wood, especially in winter, and enjoy sport with the rifle all day long, taking tree shots at the birds which fly in to rest, or feed on the acorns still on the oaks.

It will be seen how varied, and interesting, are the different methods of shooting pigeons. Wherever there is ground with pigeon on it and to which the sportsman has access, he should never be without some sport.

CHAPTER 8

# *Rock-Dove Shooting*

In the Protection of Birds Act, 1954, there is a schedule in which are listed the species of wild birds which may be killed or taken at any time by authorized persons. The schedule contains, of course, the stock-dove and the wood-pigeon. The rock-dove is also mentioned, with the provision, in brackets, 'in Scotland only'. The rock-dove is also the subject of another exception. Under Section 5 sub-section 3, of the said Act it is an offence, subject to a very severe penalty, to use 'any mechanically propelled vehicle or boat or any aircraft in immediate pursuit of a wild bird for the purpose of driving, killing or taking that bird'. It is, however, provided that 'nothing in this sub-section shall make unlawful the use (in Scotland only) of a mechanically propelled boat for the purpose of killing or taking rock-doves'.

From this it might be gathered that the rock-dove, in England and Wales and Northern Ireland is either in danger of extinction or so useful a bird that it is not necessary to shoot it. In actual fact there are considerable numbers of rock-doves round the British coasts, particularly in East Yorkshire on Flamborough Head; once the venue for many sportsmen who are now, alas, deprived of their legitimate sport of rock-dove shooting.

Undoubtedly, however, the cream of rock-dove shooting takes place in Scotland, particularly in the Western Isles. The birds nest in caverns and clefts in the steep cliffs which line the sea-lochs, and there are usually only two methods of approaching them. You either come in to them by boat from the sea, or attempt to shoot them from above. The latter is a dizzy business and it is difficult to retrieve the birds which are hit. Sometimes it is possible to get along the foot of a cliff and shoot from a narrow strip of rocks or sand, but the sportsman has to beware of the fast-running tides and be keenly sensible of the danger of being cut off and drowned.

For approach from the sea it is essential to use a motor-boat. The sea-lochs are subject to sudden squalls and gusts and manoeuvring close inshore in a rowing dinghy or sailing craft could easily mean disaster. Furthermore, it is essential to engage the services of a boatman who knows the coast intimately and understands the local weather. What one moment may be a calm sea with a clear sky can, in a matter of minutes, become an angry, rushing, tumbling mass of angry water, with a sky black as pitch, and visibility reduced to a hundered yards or less. Equally sudden is the calm which follows, when the sea becomes smooth and mirror-like. There are occasions when there is a deep swell, perhaps not apparent to the stranger to the district. The trip out in the boat may be extremely pleasant, the rise and fall of the swell hardly noticeable, yet the rise and fall of the swell may be ten or more feet (about three metres) and it needs little imagination to see what could happen if a stranger ran his craft close inshore. The keel which could pass in safety at the height of the swell with five or even ten feet to spare may, the next moment, be brought down heavily on sharp and jagged rocks. The first essential therefore when rock-pigeon shooting in Scotland, is a good local boatman who knows the coast and understands 'doo' shooting.

When the birds fly out from the cliffs they generally drop in a steep dive, level out and streak away. But this may vary according to the strength and direction of the wind. I have known birds soar out of their caverns and sweep in the updraught high over the cliff top and backwards over the land behind in but the twinkling of an eye. Certainly in even less time that it takes the boatman to accept the proffered flask.

Add to this the difficulty of maintaining balance and shooting from a platform which is rising and falling, and the difficulties of the sport will be appreciated. I have found that the most successful way of shooting rock-doves from a boat is by 'snap-shooting'. In this method the gun is fired almost at the instant it touches the shoulder. The eye is lined up on the bird and the sportsman is not conscious of seeing his barrels at all. Speed is the essential. A more open boring than full-choke is necessary for this form of shooting and the birds must be taken well within range wherever possible.

Rock-doves can be decoyed in to the fields of the crofts, but this is not a popular method of shooting: for a real thrill, shoot from the boats. A word of advice on this difficult art may not be amiss. Firstly, make sure that the gun is unloaded, better still in its case, when both boarding and disembarking. Secondly, do not load until you are in the immediate vicinity of the shooting. Thirdly, get ahead of the boatman, well up in the bows, for the shooting and on no account shoot at more than right angles to the craft. Fourthly, keep your gun barrels pointed up the whole time: should there be an accidental discharge and the gun is pointing downwards, the shot charge may pass through the side or bottom of the boat. Such things have been known to happen, and the consequences can be left to the imagination.

When the gun is not in use it should be unloaded and placed in such a position that it cannot receive damage by falling against seats or other objects. The man who lays his gun against the gunwale is asking for trouble: the movement of the boat may cause it to slip. If unloaded, the stock may be scratched or the barrels may be dented: if loaded, it may be discharged.

Cartridges should be kept in a waterproof box or tin, handy for immediate use. There is generally, even on a calm day, a certain amount of spray coming aboard a small boat and swollen cartridges which will either not go into the breech or eject from it, do not make for a pleasant day, better still use plastic cartridges.

An essential item of equipment is a long-handled landing net with which to retrieve birds from the water.

The beauty about rock-dove shooting from a boat, in the Western Isles at any rate, is that one can cruise down several miles of miniature fjords, taking shots all the time, and enjoying a continual change of scenery coupled with the exhilarating tang of the sea air. Certainly no other form of shooting can provide this. I have often cruised for distances up to ten miles in pursuit of the fast, wild rock-dove.

In an earlier chapter I have remarked about colonies of rock-doves round the English and Welsh coasts and also inland, frequenting cliffs, as well as the disused quarry workings near industrial centres. To all intents and purposes these birds, by habit, by plumage, by flight, are genuine rock-doves. However, under the Protection of Birds Act, 1954, it is not lawful to shoot rock-doves in the British Isles outside of Scotland.

It would appear therefore that the shooting of the inland rock-doves would be illegal. However, the shooting man, despite his disagreement with the findings of ornithologists in connection with the winter invasion of wood-pigeons, has cause to bless the same naturalists. It is the general opinion amongst most ornithologists that these colonies of rock-doves are not in fact true rock-doves, but domestic pigeons which have gone wild and by generations of breeding, reverted back to type. An analogy may be seen in the case of our wild goats which, our naturalists assert, are not really wild but domestic animals gone feral. In the Second Schedule to the Protection of Birds Act, 1954, amongst the wild birds which may be taken or killed at any time by authorized persons appears 'Domestic pigeon gone feral'. This, it may safely be assumed, applies to the so-called 'rock-doves' (I do not mean, of course, the stock-doves) of our inland precipices and quarries. So a splendid sporting proposition is opened up to the sportsman who has a colony of such birds on his shooting ground. In spite of their descent from domestic stock these birds are extremely difficult to approach, far more wary in fact than their cousins the wood-pigeons.

But, before discussing inland rock-dove shooting (and this applies to all pigeon shooting) the sportsman should study the wording of the Act relating to 'authorized persons', discover what are the qualifications of such persons, and how the requisite authority is obtained.

To begin with, in the interpretation clauses to the said Act (Section 14, sub-section 1) – 'authorized person' means:

'(*a*) the owner or occupier, or any person shown to have been authorized by the owner or occupier, of any land on which the action authorized is taken;

'(*b*) any person authorized in writing by the local authority for the area within which the action authorized is taken;

'(*c*) any person authorized in writing by any of the following bodies, that is to say, the Nature Conservancy, a river board constituted under the River Boards Act, 1948, a local fisheries committee constituted under the Sea Fisheries Regulation Act, 1888, the Conservators of the River Thames, the Lee Conservancy Catchment Board, any statutory water undertakers within the meaning of the Water Act, 1945, any local water authority within the meaning of the Water (Scotland) Act, 1946, the Commissioners appointed under the Tweed Fisheries Act, 1857, and the district board for a fishery district within the meaning of the Salmon Fisheries (Scotland) Act, 1863;

'so, however, that the authorization of any person for the purposes that this definition shall not confer any right of entry upon any land;

' "occupier", in relation to any land other than the foreshore, includes any person having any right of hunting, shooting, fishing or taking game or fish.'

From the foregoing it does not appear to be necessary for the sportsman to hold written permission from the occupier of lands, e.g. a farmer or market gardener, unless the land is held by, or permission obtained from, the authorities in paragraphs (*b*) and (*c*) to the sub-section quoted. The mere granting of verbal permission will be sufficient authority. Even so the sportsman would be well advised, to avoid all arguments, to get the grantor to put the permission in writing. A simple letter is sufficient, and this should not be difficult to obtain, though some countrymen are rather averse to putting their signature to anything in writing in case they bind themselves unnecessarily.

Before commencing operations against inland rock-doves (I am using that term for domestic pigeon gone feral, as being less unwieldy), the shooter must reconnoitre thoroughly the area which is to be the scene of his campaign. Conditions may vary so greatly that perhaps a brief description of some of my inland rock-dove shooting forays would be better than trying to lay down hard and fast rules for this form of sport.

A year or so before the last war I had permission to shoot over some rough moorland in the Pennines. Within sight of the shoot the black chimneys of the textile mills thrust into the air and from their mouths belched soot and grime which blackened and stained the moorland grasses and the small crops of heather which struggled for a foothold there. Yet, in spite of the proximity of the towns and the hordes of week-end hikers and ramblers which spewed over the great hills, snipe and curlew, peewits and golden plover nested there. Hares, the quarry of the miners with their long dogs and whippets, abounded and here, secure against lines of beaters pushing them towards concealed guns, the hill partridges passed their lives in comparative peace. Adjoining the rough moorland was a small farm, indeed the description 'croft' would have suited it better, and from the poor earth the dalesman and his wife scratched a living. This farm was my headquarters and on the near-by reservoir, which supplied water to a factory in the valley below, I used to watch the oyster-catchers in their spring nuptials, and sometimes in the late summer a party of migrant shelduck rested there for a while. At one end of the moor there was a great quarry. Once the stones had shone with the faint gold of the sandstone, but years of exposure to the elements and to the drifting smoke from the tall chimneys had reduced them to an indeterminate grey-brown and black. The quarry, disused, since the growth of the brick industry, had brought stone building to an end in that part of the world, was divided into a series of large holes in the bottom of which lay tangled heaps of rusty machinery, derelict buildings, piles of stones, and dressed 'flags'. Two of the holes were filled with bright green water, of a depth which had to be imagined, and one of them was reputed to be haunted by the earth-bound spirits of two suicides who had drowned themselves there. Amongst the rubbish and tangled rusty irons, grey rabbits lived, and high up in the quarry walls there were several colonies of rock-doves.

Time and time again the farmer, and other local sportsmen had waged war against these pigeons but, apart from odd birds, success was nil. Indeed, until I arrived on the scene, the birds were written off as unapproachable and unshootable. It was impossible to approach them from the moor top: the moment a shooter got near the edge the pigeons would vanish out of the quarry from the other side. It was difficult, even dangerous, to try and climb down to a platform, so flighting them was ruled out. It was possible to stalk along the quarry paths themselves, but impossible to get near enough to shoot them as they took off from the cliff sides. And as for waiting up in the quarry: birds hit, more often than not, fell into the deep holes from which they could not be recovered, or were lost in the crevices of the huge piles of stones.

The subject was mentioned to me one evening when, after a most successful day with the snipe, the farmer had said: 'How about them pigeons?'

'They say they're impossible,' I countered, 'and from what I've seen I don't think they're worth spending a lot of time over: while I've got snipe and partridge, and the odd rabbit, why should I waste time over them?'

'My old dad, he usta get 'em: never could hit no snipe,' said the dalesman. 'Reckon tha could do it if tha tried.' Then he winked at me as he filled his pipe. 'Of course, they do say as 'ow it can't be done. Reckon, on second thoughts, tha'd never do it.'

The challenge was there and had to be accepted.

I spent several days studying the layout of the quarry. I studied the approach. I watched the way the birds entered and left. I tried to stalk them and always they beat me. But all these excursions were carried out without a gun. Finally, I decided I had seen enough and it was time to go into action. I had, in the meantime, culled all the information I could about these pigeons from the various sportsmen I knew who had tried to come to terms with them. 'No good,' was their inevitable answer, 'you can't get near them and if you do you don't get much of a shot. If you do hit one it's ten to one it'll be lost in the quarry.'

The first, and most important, factor I discovered about these birds, and a rule which applies to rock-pigeons wherever you may shoot them, was that when alarmed they flew out *downwind* at the first opportunity. No matter where the birds were resting in the quarry, they would, when alarmed, drop from their ledge and plunge towards the bottom, then they would turn and climb rapidly leaving the quarry top downwind. With that point kept in mind procedure was simple enough. All I had to do was to place myself in position some twenty yards or more downwind from the quarry lip, and hide in either a natural hollow or in a shallow pit which I had dug. Safely in position I then hurled a small stone into the quarry so that it clattered on the stones below. Within a couple of seconds of the stone dropping into the quarry the pigeon would come clattering out downwind and right over me. I had some pretty shots that way as a startled pigeon whipping downwind takes plenty of swing, but I was invariably successful and I can honestly claim that, if the pigeons were in the quarry, I would nearly always bring back at least a couple. As a result of this I acquired a reputation, which I scarcely deserved, as a crack pigeon shot. Of course, when I started to bring home the pigeons the other gunners wanted to try and there was considerable activity on that moor until the locals decided to call it an unprofitable day. As there was so much unrestricted shooting there, being open to all, I kept my method a secret, otherwise the birds would have been decimated and the survivors probably driven away.

I also obtained some good bags amongst these birds in the early summer, setting out a field of decoys on the cotton grasses, about 100 yards (91 m) from the quarry edge. The birds on approaching or leaving the quarries would often come in to my decoys and never seemed to grow any wiser. At that time decoying of pigeon was looked upon as a magic art, and few could be prevailed upon to try it out.

Nearly all rock-doves take that splendid dive when launching themselves from the cliffs and it is very pretty shooting to catch them at the bottom of this swoop before they commence to climb.

## ROCK-DOVE SHOOTING

Of all pigeons, the rock-dove provides the hardest type of shooting: they are fast and I think that they test the sportsman's skill to the utmost. One rock-dove fairly shot is worth a dozen woodies.

## CHAPTER 9

# *Where to Shoot?*

Probably the greatest problem which confronts the average shooting man today is that of 'Where may I shoot?' The wildfowler has, of course, access to a vast acreage of free saltings and foreshore, but the inland sportsman has either to rent a shoot by himself or in a syndicate with others, or avail himself of those opportunities offered by the very excellent sporting hotels which abound in these islands.

The renting of shoots is difficult in areas within easy reach of large towns on account of the great number of sportsmen who want to take part and the limited amount of shooting available. Furthermore the rents are often far too high, altogether out of proportion to the shooting offered.

The artisan gunner, in particular, must make the most of his opportunities. Personally, I have built up a large acreage of shooting without the payment of any rent, as such, at all. Rents have been in the form of the odd bird or rabbit given to the farmer from time to time, the provision of cigarettes or tobacco, the odd drink, and most important of all the rendering of services in kind to the farmer. Such services may be helping to rewire a fence, informing him of sick or dead stock, performing minor mechanical operations on the numerous vehicles which now abound on farms, and so on. The filling in of forms and assistance in the drafting of letters are services which the clerk can use to overcome any prejudice the farmer may have in 'letting' his shooting. More often than not, however, there will be no 'letting' as such: the actual shooting will be 'by permission'. Many farmers like to shoot themselves and in several instances are loath to let their shoots, besides, they like the independence of giving 'permission to shoot', which may be withdrawn at any time.

The greatest number of sportsmen interested in shooting pigeon will be those who are 'shootless'. As the man who can afford to rent a shoot will have the help of either an estate agent or a reasonable bank manager, there is no need for me to explain how to go about it. The remarks in this chapter are, therefore, devoted to those who are not endowed overplentifully with this world's goods.

The first, and most difficult, item is to find a farmer or market gardener willing to grant you permission to shoot over his land. The would-be pigeon shooter must not imagine that he can approach any farmer and in so many words introduce himself as the answer to the farmer's prayer as a destroyer of marauding pigeons. He must realize the farmer's point of view. That view is dependent upon one word – TRUST. By what right, can you, a perfect stranger, expect any landowner to allow you, a stranger from an urban area, loose on his lands? Put yourself in the farmer's position and you will appreciate that. Furthermore, no farmer, nor any countryman for that matter, likes to be told, 'Let me do this and I'll be doing you a good turn.' The idea of favours lavished upon him is repugnant to him. Your countryman, no matter how slow he may appear to the townsman, no matter how (apparently) shabbily dressed, or queerly spoken, is by nature proud. The farmer is apt to think: 'He says he is doing me a favour – what's he getting out of me? How much shall I lose in the long run?' It is much better to gain the farmer's confidence. This may mean long, perhaps boring, talks in the local hostelry, over the gate, in the roadside, about crops and weather prospects for agriculture, fowl pest, foot-and-mouth disease, myxomatosis, the Test Match or local football team. Finally, the talks, perhaps after several days, will be brought down to the subject of pigeons and vermin and the damage done to crops. Let the farmer volunteer the information that the pigeons have ruined a field of peas, then is your time to introduce yourself. Suggest that there would be nothing you would like better than a *day* after them with the gun. This permission will probably be forthcoming. 'Any time you like,' will probably be the answer. The next thing is to ascertain the correct boundaries of the shooting area, and to do this it is as well to ask permission to walk round *without* the gun, and get the farmer (if he has time and is willing) to accompany you and to show you where the greatest havoc by pigeons has been committed. Finally, ask his permission to make hides, or dig pits, before you commence to do so.

It is as well to restrain yourself on your first foray under these conditions. Try only to take certain shots so that you can bring back a reasonable bag of birds to display before the farmer. Offer him his share, and next time you call round inform him of the crop contents. This is in order to keep him informed as to whether or not they have been damaging his crops, as if the crops are full of clover and he has no clover on his ground, the pigeon are raiding elsewhere. He will probably tell you in such circumstances that the next farm has clover crops and suggest you call there. In time you can build up a reasonable shoot over three or four such farms. But never forget that you are on trust and that that trust must never be betrayed.

Observe the country code. Do not trample growing crops. Do not bring dogs on to land without the farmer's permission. Do not scare livestock or poultry. Remember to close gates. Observe local prejudices, not shooting on a Sunday, for example, and do not bring strangers on to the land without asking the permission of the farmer beforehand. All this sounds trite, but unless you obey such simple rules, you will soon find yourself without any shooting. Furthermore the 'bush telegraph' will convey your name and description around the locality, and other farmers will politely, but firmly, decline your offers to shoot harmful birds, whether such offers are accompanied by monetary inducements or otherwise.

It may well be, however, that in spite of all his approaches, which have been well received by the farmers concerned, the sportsman has still been unable to find any shooting. There may be a multitude of reasons for this, but the chief one will probably be that the shooting has already been let.

Formerly the sportsman could avail himself of the opportunities which were presented to him by the campaign against pigeons (and other harmful birds) which was organized by the Ministry of Agriculture through the pest officers.

The pest officer kept a register of *bona fide* pigeon and harmful bird shots, and organized 'pigeon drives' and arranged for parties of guns to attend certain areas. At organized shoots cartridges were available to the sportsmen concerned at half-price, and reduced-rate cartridges were also available to the registered shot. Some agricultural executive committees put the sportsman in touch with farmers who had requested assistance: others issued to the successful applicant a letter of introduction which had to be presented as evidence of his genuineness when contacting farmers.

Reduced-price cartridges were issued on the understanding that they would be used only for the destruction of harmful birds, namely, wood-pigeons, stock-doves, carrion crows, rooks and jackdaws, and the *bona fide* registered pigeon shooter was placed 'on his honour' not to use them for any other purpose, nor to shoot anything else.

Where an agricultural executive committee introduced a registered shot to a farmer, it acted only in an introductory capacity and in its covering letter generally stated that:

1. The A.E.C. concerned would not be held responsible for any incident, injury or damage caused by the shooting and
2. Shotguns only to be used: rifles of any description were strictly forbidden.

In many cases, the introduction effected by these means did result in the sportsman being told by the farmer to 'come and shoot any time you like' and quite often the shot was given permission to shoot rabbits, and even game.

Unfortunately the scheme does not apply today and the keen shooter is exhorted to shoot wood-pigeons with expensive, full-price cartridges which also carry value added tax. So much for the wisdom of government departments!

Today, failing a direct approach to a farmer, the best way to obtain pigeon shooting is either to join a well-organized pigeon club or wildfowling association. Of course, such a club may have restricted membership and this will mean that the applicant has to go on to a waiting list.

Frankly, I prefer to join a pigeon club rather than a wildfowling association. Typical clubs of this nature, and models on which new bodies are advised to pattern themselves are the Midlands Wood-Pigeon Club, and the Middlesex Wood-Pigeon Club. This latter, operating in the region of London, is very successful and a very good example of how such a club should be run.

If there is no wildfowling association or pigeon club which the would-be shooter can join, then it is worthwhile his considering trying to form a small club! This is not quite so difficult as it sounds. There are always a number of shooters without shooting grounds and a discreet advertisement in a sporting paper, or locally, will usually result in a small number of men getting together to discuss the possibility of such a club coming into being. Most of these informal clubs, generally with a membership of about twelve, are based on some local inn. Under the title of a club organized to assist in vermin control, with proper constitution and rules, it is easier to approach farmers. It is also easier to satisfy farmers because there are the occasions when one of two sportsmen just cannot cope with the pigeons adequately and as killing pigeons must be done to the satisfaction of the farmer, a club can put more members into the field at a given time to ensure success.

The rules should provide for expulsion of members for dangerous or unsportsmanlike conduct, and should always include an insurance scheme for its members.

Wildfowling associations are not the best media in which to come to terms with the wood-pigeons. Firstly they generally have a restricted membership, secondly when members should be helping the farmers against pigeons the shooters are off down to the coast after ducks and geese! Again, many wildfowl clubs enforce a rule that members must also be full members of the Wildfowlers' Association of Great Britain and Ireland. This is an extension of the 'closed-shop' principle. As some wildfowling clubs have increased their activities to include rough shooting and pigeon shooting, even extending over farms which formerly were shot over by individuals with the kindness of the farmer, such individuals have found their shooting gone and, owing to restricted membership rules, unable to enjoy their sport!

Unfortunately many so-called wildfowlers are looking for an odd day's shooting. I have had a lot of experience of this when, following promises from wildfowling clubs by writing to farmers or calling upon them that they would tackle their pigeons freely, I have gone along and shown the shooters where the birds are feeding or likely to feed, placed them in the best shooting positions, and then retired to a less advantageous spot myself. In every case except one, the wildfowlers have been intent on shooting the birds they can see in their immediate vicinity, and time and time again I have seen approaching flocks veer away because the wildfowler has shot at the first arrival. Again I have noted a tendency for shots to be taken at and beyond extreme range and though I have coaxed and even pleaded first of all get as near to the birds you can and then let them get nearer to you, over enthusiam has ended up in long range shooting, a waste of cartridges, and a very poor bag.

Again, none of the promises were fulfilled when the farmers wanted pigeon shot at short notice, and though undoubtedly those who did take part in these shoots enjoyed themselves, they were of little value to the farmer, and a bit of a nuisance to the local shooter who depends upon the pigeon for his sport.

Frankly, though restricted membership should apply to small clubs, which are really syndicates, it is better for wildfowling clubs to operate a restricted shooting rule rather than a restricted membership. It is better for 100 members to shoot in rotation, a total of, say, 200 days than 25 members to shoot a total of, say 400 days.,

In any event, for the sake of the sport generally, I think that pigeon clubs, even small syndicates, should affiliate to the national bodies such as the British Field Sports Society and the Wildfowlers' Association ofGreat Britain and Ireland: and if the individual desires, should join these bodies as a member in his own right without pressure of a club rule.

Cost of ammunition is a very important consideration for the pigeon shooter. Many forays may only result in a few shots being fired, but there are occasions when the hordes of marauding pigeons mean a vast expenditure of cartridges! Shooting the odd bird for the pot is one thing, but trying to cope with hundreds of pigeons bent on feeding on a particular spot is another. Perhaps 500, or even more, cartridges may be fired by one shooter in one day. Now the first duty of the pigeon shooter is to the farmer over whose land he is shooting, either by trying to kill as many pigeons as possible or scaring them away (which latter is rather a Canute-ish effort).

Of course, the shot birds can be sold and the proceeds put towards the expenses of shooting them.

Enter the pigeon shooters' co-operative. This simply means a banding together of three or four sportsmen and using their limited ammunition in the best possible way. Obviously four guns firing 25 rounds each can cover a given area better than one gun firing 100 rounds. A rota system can be used whereby the man who has had a good stand can exchange with one whose stand is less exciting. This ensures that crops are properly protected against the pigeons, the farmer is being cared for, and each shooter is getting a worthwhile share of this wonderful sport.

When applying to a pigeon club for registration the applicant should state his qualifications. Naturally enough the authority concerned wants to have some details of the sportsman's experience and bona fides otherwise a whole mob of poachers and gun lunatics would be entered on their files. When replying, in first instance, the secretary will probably, though not in all cases, send the applicant a form to complete. This generally asks for details of shooter's experience, the methods he uses to shoot pigeons and other harmful birds, whether or not he is a member of some other club, the type of gun he uses, and whether or not he already holds written permission to shoot over land. This last seems an almost impossible obstacle to surmount so far as the shootless sportsman is concerned, but if he points out to the secretary that he is a keen safe shot (probably quoting membership of a grey squirrel club, a wildfowlers' club, or some similar body) but has no shoot of his own and at the same time gives details of lands over which he has shot, perhaps as a guest, he may satisfy the questioner. There is a saying in the legal profession that hard cases make bad law: there has to be some line drawn somewhere, and it must be realized by the sportsman that the pigeon club and the other members must have some form of protection for their good names. Never must it be forgotten that the aims and objects of enrolling as a bona fide pigeon shot are not just to provide sport for the applicant: whatever sport comes his way is incidental, he is enrolling on a pest control operation. The whole aim and object of this scheme is to bring pigeons under control, to assist the farmers, and to help the country in its food production.

The man who wishes to register just for the sake of an odd afternoon's shooting is unfair to the association, to the farmer, and to his fellow citizens. Furthermore, he is probably filling a place in a list which has no vacancy for a bona fide person, who really wishes to assist in the drive against the feathered foes of agriculture.

Pest control, and this includes pigeon shooting, is a national service, and it should be in that spirit that the sportsman requests registration as a harmful-bird shooter. The fact that the recruit enjoys the work has no bearing on the objects of that work.

Unfortunately there is a type of shooter (I will not dub him sportsman) who seeks to enrol as a bona fide pigeon shot in order to obtain introductions to farmers and others. Armed with such an introduction he then tries to tempt the farmer into letting the shooting to him exclusively. He is after a shoot by hook or by crook. I recall vividly just such an instance. I had finished an afternoon's sport on one of the farms I visit and was standing at the farm doorway, talking to my friend the farmer, when a big car rolled into the farmyard. A well-clad, obviously well-nourished, and well-wadded man descended from the car and approached us. He flourished a letter from the local agricultural executive committee which stated that he had been appointed a bona fide pigeon shot and asked if he could shoot the pigeons.

'Certainly,' replied the farmer. 'Almost any time you like.'

'Any game?' was the next question.

'A little,' was the guarded reply.

'Give you twenty pounds for the season,' said the opulent one, making ready to open his wallet.

'Twenty pounds? What for?' asked my friend, winking at me.

'Your shooting. Make it thirty, then. It isn't let, is it?' The last question a little anxiously.

'Well, yes it is, as a matter of fact,' said the farmer.

'Now I'll tell you what I'll do,' went on the visitor, 'I'll give you ten pounds now to hold the shoot for me, and pay you thirty for next season, and in the meantime I suppose it'll be all right for me to shoot a few pigeon.'

'Listen, mister,' said the farmer, and he reverted to his native dialect, 'I've let t'shoot for nowt, see.'

'Nowt?'

This was some long time ago, as £20 would not go very far today. It was, in fact, in 1954. But the mentality of these gentlemen is still unchanged.

'What my friend means,' I cut in, 'is that he lets the shoot to friends for nothing.'

'Good heavens man, I'm offering you . . .'

'If you give me a hundred quid it wouldn't do no good,' said my friend, 'You'd shoot a couple of pigeon here and there, knock off all my partridges and then forget me the next year. I know, I've had some. No, what I want is someone to come on and clear them damned woodies off my land. I let the local shooters on, they get plenty enough of birds, and they don't do no harm. Still, you can come and shoot them pigeons whenever you want.'

Deflated, the financier pushed his wallet back and went back to his car. We watched him drive off. 'He'll never come back,' I remarked. 'He couldn't care less about shooting pigeons.'

I was right. We never saw him again.

The farmer was quite right in his attitude. One gun, or two, paying a high rent would not meet his problem. What he wanted was several guns, continually on his land, killing the birds or driving them elsewhere.

From February until the end of March in each year is the period for organized shoots against pigeons. These take place over various lands, including large shooting estates, where the head keeper generally organizes the campaign. Such shoots are generally held on

Saturdays, with midweek shoots on Thursdays and Wednesdays. It has been estimated that, annually over 2,250,000 pigeons are shot at these organized shoots! Count also the number of pigeon shot by individual shooters and sporting parties, which are not reported to the Ministry of Agriculture and you get a fair idea of the amount of shooting which pigeon can stand, for their numbers seem little decreased.

A little advice about these organized shoots is perhaps necessary for the man who has previously shot either alone or in the company of one or two friends. In the first place be on time. Secondly, if humanly possible, do turn up. Nothing is worse for organizers than to be faced with shooting delayed through late arrivals, or too small a number of guns turning up to cover a decent-sized wood.

When placed in position do not move from it until told to do so. The organizers of the shoot have carefully placed every man not only with a view to doing the greatest damage to the pigeons, but also in order to avoid damage to the shooters through careless gun handling. If you move to another position, you may place yourself in the line of fire of some other gun, or you yourself find a third party on the end of your own barrels. Quite often at these organized shoots, rabbits and foxes are on the permitted list and low aimed shots may well cause casualties if shooters move about indiscriminately.

When in position do not carry on loud conversation with your neighbour or neighbours. In spite of the fact that pigeons have better eyesight than hearing, their hearing is nevertheless acute, and the human voice carries far and soon warns the birds of impending danger.

Allow the birds to come well in before shooting. Even if others tackle high birds at impossible heights, do not emulate them. If they wish to waste powder and shot it is up to them: you are there to kill pigeons, not expend half-price cartridges needlessly. Do not shoot at a bird which is coming to another gun. These are simple little rules the observance of which is easy. They make for safety and success in the shooting field.

If crows and pigeons abound it is your duty to shoot *both*. Do not neglect the crows for the sake of a pigeon in the pot, and do not shoot foxes unless expressly authorized to do so. You may be in hunting country, so remember your duty to your fellow sportsmen and keep the bead on feathered targets!

Out of such organized shoots may very well come invitations to attend other, non-official shoots, or invitations from farmers to shoot over their land whenever you like. But these invitations will depend as much on your behaviour as on your prowess with the gun.

It is permissible to take your lofting decoys with you and place them in position near your stand. In this manner, by forgetting about the other shooters, and concentrating on the task ahead as if you were shooting alone, you will find that your day will be attended with success. Few men, especially if not previously experienced in shooting before an audience, can perform well when thrust into a group of strangers. There is the feeling, 'I mustn't muff this shot,' or 'Oh dear, I hope I do all right'. It is quite a natural feeling because most shooters, in secret if not in public, like to feel that they are moderately skilled. They are apt to become edgy and nervous when asked to shoot before spectators, themselves shooting men, and as a result cannot concentrate on the task in hand, miss a few shots, lose confidence and go to pieces.

Forget about the other men. Concentrate on your bird. Do not worry about whether you will hit it or miss it, just go about the job calmly and when you pull off your favourite shot – perhaps a high overhead, or a jinking going away – let that glow go through you, but do not let the compliment, 'Well done, old man,' from your neighbour, go to your head. If you let it affect you you will be tempted to try an impossible shot, miss it, and thereafter fluff an easy bird and go to pieces.

If you turn up at an organized shoot on some large estate where the sportsmen are better equipped than yourself (perhaps beautiful guns costing a few thousand pounds are to be seen) do not feel ashamed for your humble, machine-made single. It is your gun, you shoot well with it, you enjoy yourself with it, and there is no earthly reason why man for man you should not do as well as the better armed fellow.

In brief, be yourself: keep cool: keep well behaved: retain your confidence. Not only will you be invited again, many doors in the shooting world will be opened to you. Nothing succeeds in sport like sportsmanship.

CHAPTER 10

# *Sporting Days*

---

It is very important that the pigeon shooter should keep a shooting diary. It is also an act of courtesy to inform the person over whose land you shoot, of your bags from time to time: say twice in a season. A member of a pigeon shooting club may find that it is a condition of membership that he makes regular and accurate returns of birds he has shot.

When making such a return be most careful only to enter birds which have actually been killed: that is, birds collected. Lost birds and wounded birds should not find a place in these statistics.

The shooting diary to which I have referred is the sportsman's own personal history of his shooting life. Too often a small pocket-book has bare details entered in it in various columns. Game diaries of the past, and present, are apt to degenerate into mere shooting book-keeping, consisting of columns of figures for different species shot, coupled with names and dates. That is not a shooting diary: it is a single-entry shooting journal at the end of which a balance sheet is made.

A quarto or foolscap notebook makes an ideal shooting diary. Let one page be ruled into columns if the sportsman so desires, into which the various bags and dates may be entered, but let there be other pages devoted to a minor history of each day's sport. No matter how small the amount of sport a brief picture of it can be given. Items such as the type of weather, the crops, other species of birds seen, the way the pigeons flew, the shots which missed as well as the shots which told, should all be entered. Not only does it make pleasant reading at a later date, but often forms the nucleus of intelligence for future excursions, perhaps even the nucleus for a sporting article or a book. Memory is fallible and cannot be relied upon. In retrospect only the good occasions are remembered and the sportsman is given to 'If only——' in his ruminations.

It is a good idea to make a small map of your shoot upon which the different flight lines, according to weather conditions or cropping operations, may be recorded. On such a map it is also possible to plan sites for hides and pits and then survey your plans against the actual background.

The following are extracts from my own shooting journals, and, if I introduce a personal note, I trust that I will be forgiven as I hope through these incidents to give the sportsman some idea of different aspects of pigeon shooting.

*February in Berkshire*

It was a grim winter. The roads were frostbound and snowbound while on the coast great blocks of ice formed on the foreshore. The few waders which I shot in these artic conditions were nothing but skin and bone, and one poor curlew which I put out of its misery, was tottering about on the edge of the tide, scarcely able to stand, unable to fly, with its breastbone sticking through the skin.

'Come over to my place and have a go at the pigeon;' Colin Willock of ITV 'Survival' fame, whom I was teaching wildfowling and introducing to the world of muzzle-loaders, knowing of my keenness for pigeon shooting had invited me over the telephone. I hesitated, the conditions were bad and it was unlikely that any pigeon would be present on his shoot, and even if present, hardly worth powder and shot.

'They were in in hundreds a couple of days ago.' Colin was insistent, so I agreed.

His shoot was rather unusual in layout in that it consisted of a belt of land bordering a large lake of about fifty acres (20·2 ha). In the centre of the lake was a small well-wooded island to which the pigeon flocked to roost, and to breed. The actual depth of the shoot round this water was about 300 yards (275 m) but it was a goodly circumference. The whole was well-wooded with both deciduous trees and evergreens, there were small patches of bracken-covered slopes, and two fields which jutted into the circle.

After a somewhat hazardous journey by car we reached the shoot and saw the tops of the tall firs filled with pigeons. Hungry thirsty coots sat in disconsolate groups in the centre of the track winding round the lake, and refused to move before our vehicle, until one bold bird dashed for the ice, slipped, skidded, and was blown downwind in a crazy waltz in the undignified position of feet in the air, rotating upon whatever passes for a bird's sit-upon. In the centre of the lake a vast flock of mixed wildfowl – wigeon, mallard, pochard, and tufted duck – stood motionless, no preening of feathers, no movement of heads. But the pigeons continued in a long passage to and from the island, in and out of the tree branches, keeping up a constant movement to some fields of roots lying half a mile or so beyond the shoot.

We tossed for position. Colin decided to take the upwind side of the lake and try to walk up a few pigeons in the trees, take a few shots at the grey squirrel which abounded, and then put himself in position for the evening flight. I decided to position myself in a clearing in the wood itself, on one of the flight lines to the central island.

The sun was brilliant and I longed for a pair of tinted glasses. It shone from a clear, pale blue sky, reflecting on the white snow-covered fields, which sparkled like diamonds, and gave off an intense and uncomfortable glare. I think that was the factor which decided me to seek a spot in the wood from which to shoot. Shooting against that glare would not only be bad for the eyes but would make it difficult to spot approaching birds.

After diligent exploration I found the clearing I desired. The trees were set very closely together, and there was considerable undergrowth, but the spot I chose had a space in the trees which was large enough for me to come to terms with pigeons flying across it. Perhaps the space between the tree tops was twenty yards (18·29 m) certainly no more. At the rear of the clearing stood a dead oak and as I entered the wood I saw a pigeon sitting high up among the leafless trees. A brief, breathless stalk brought me up against the tree hole and immediately beneath him. The ensuing vertical sitting shot brought my first pigeon into the bag, though without much elation. Turning my attention to the possibility of a hide, I noticed that heavy though the snow had been for the past few days, the bracken in the wood was barely covered. It was but a matter of moments to build a reasonable stook of bracken on a blackberry bush, which was growing against the trunk of a fallen tree.

I made my hide in the form of a letter 'P', so that I was covered from all sides, yet had a little passage through which I might enter and return after picking up dead birds. I placed my cartridges handy, laid my gun in front of me on the tree trunk, then added a touch of bracken to my hat, and waited.

The waiting period was remarkably short. Within a matter of minutes a couple of pigeons topped the row of trees in front of me and had passed right over my head. Through the leafless twigs I could see a long line of pigeons making for the island, upwind of me and behind me. Gently I eased the gun into a ready position and waited. The first birds topped the trees slightly to my left and were impossible to shoot at as they vanished almost immediately into the arc of the woody circle enclosing me. However, I could see the movement of wings coming in to me and bringing the gun up into my shoulder was able to snap two quick shots at a pair of woodies as they broke across my clearing. At the reports the following line split up and divided before it reached me and I watched two plump wood-pigeon, followed by a miniature snowfall of feathers, plunge down into the undergrowth behind me. As they fell they hit the branches of the smaller trees and brought miniature cascades of snow tumbling in their wake.

As I retrieved my birds, which were only about five paces from the rear of my hide, I heard Colin's gun boom and within half a minute a flock of about fifty birds streaked downwind, over my head, but at an impossible height. I slid into my hide and watched them wheel and turn, then, as one bird they swooped in dive-bomber tactics, head into wind, towards the old tree behind me, I made the fatal mistake of trying to shoot the leaders. I should have let the first birds settle in the tree and then taken the others. Unfortunately my enthusiasm overruled my good sense, and I expended two barrels in vain.

There followed a brief lull, during which period I emptied the crops of the three pigeons. If they had been feeding on roots nearby, they would soon become rank and tainted. It was necessary to empty their crops if they were to provide a good dish. To my surprise they were not filled with root tops at all, they were crammed with the tips of conifers, and hips and haws from the hawthorn and dog roses which flourished around and on the shoot. Neither were the birds lean or emaciated as the wildfowl: they were rich, well-fed, plump, greedy pigeon, well worth powder and shot and the long, chilly journey over the treacherous roads.

Again the distant report of Colin's gun, and this time birds began to trickle over me in ones and twos. They afforded at least ten minutes of intermittent shooting and in this period I brought down another ten birds. One of them caught by the wind, spun down like a spinning jenny, and landed in the hide beside me. I had the mortification of seeing another beautifully killed bird drop like a stone and wedge itself immovably in the crotch of a branch at a height which I could not reach, nor would all the shaking of the tree dislodge it. This, incidentally, is not an unusual occurrence when shooting pigeons in woods and often accounts for birds seen to drop, but for which search on the ground proves unavailing.

For three hours pigeons continued to fly over my small clearing at intervals of only a few minutes, and before the end of the afternoon my stock of ammunition had been exhausted, and the pile of slain had grown. I therefore left my hide and commenced an exhaustive search for birds which I had dropped, but not gathered. They were not easy to find: some had plunged into the dense undergrowth, others were lodged in blackberry bushes some two or three feet from the ground: others were tracked by the trail of white down feathers which clung to branches and twigs, and which, now and again, shifted from their perch by an eddy in the wind, drifted along the air currents, attracting my attention to the spot where a bird was likely to be lying. But not all my dropped birds were gathered I am afraid.

With but two or three cartridges left in my pocket, I was joined by Colin who had stirred up the pigeon on the other side of the lake and added to our joint total, he had also carried on a minor campaign against the grey squirrels and flourished several tails, worth 'twelve pence each'.

Colin took my place in the hide and I stood back on the edge of the wood, taking up my stand by a decrepit gate on the farm road. To my left a tall belt of firs stretched up a steep hillside: in front of me, bounded by beeches and oaks, an empty, snow-covered field glistened into the setting sun. A couple of shots from Colin's position and I saw a pigeon crumple up and drop into him: a moment later he fired again. Then my attention was given to a stream of pigeons flying in along the tops of the firs to my left. Boldly, confidently they came in and I was raising the gun to take a bird when Colin's gun roared close by, my birds took immediate alarm and swerved off.

A minute later a second stream, headed my way, lost its leader to my right barrel. I watched my second bird close its wings then suddenly commence to climb, turn over on its back and drop dead into a clump of thick thorns. It was impossible to get at this bird. I felt in my pockets: good grief! only one cartridge left, and at that moment Colin joined me. 'Good sport!' was his comment, 'I've just fired my last round!'

'Get your bird?' I asked. He nodded. 'Good!' I said, and we turned to re-enter the wood, collect the slain, and make for the car and homewards. Just as we reached the outermost trees I spotted a single bird coming in to us. We stood motionless, trying hard to pretend to be part of the fencing. We were fully exposed to the bird but Master Pigeon came steadily on.

At the last moment, when he was about twenty-five yards (22·8 m) out, with the red blaze of the sun beneath him, I flung up the gun and blotting him out with the barrels, squeezed the trigger, detonating my one and only cartridge. The pigeon stopped dead in the air, and very obligingly pitched within a couple of feet of us.

'He certainly asked for it,' remarked Colin, 'I would not have believed a pigeon would have come in like that.' Our complete absence of movement had, of course, foxed the bird which, intent on reaching the shelter of the island, was watching the countryside *beyond* us until it was too late.

The day over, we collected our bag and empty cases (for I reload my own shells over and over again) and made for home. I won't disclose the size of the bag which should have been bigger, but it took the pair of us, and a deck-chair utilized as a stretcher, to carry them into Colin's front door. For the following week, in spite of giving birds away, both Colin's family and mine lived on pigeons roast, pigeons en casserole, fried pigeons, pigeons with olives, and in spite of all the theorists who claim that a diet of pigeons over a prolonged period will have ill effects on the eater, every member of the families concerned remained hale, hearty and in good humour.

### *August in Middlesex*

Hounslow Heath is famed for its 'Gentlemen of the Road' of a more lawless age – now it forms a pleasant recreation ground for pedestrians out to enjoy the open, though sulphur-laden, air of the Metropolis, and the plighting of troths. Almost within shooting distance is a mighty airport, from which a constant procession of aircraft comes and goes, filling the air with a monotonous drone, or a high-pitched scream. The air is never without the sight of one or more aircraft, be it a trainer, or a mighty airliner coming in from, or setting off to, the Continent. Over this same airport large bags of partridges are made every season. And over this 'countryside' of airport and tarmac, main roads and houses, open heath, and municipal refuse dump (over which, incidentally, we had one wintry day a very fine partridge drive!) is a continual coming and going of pigeons. Stock-doves and woodies mixed in flocks, domestic pigeons gone feral, and racing pigeons in small groups on fast, determined flight on a set course, present a non-stop ornithological display.

Bounded on one side by the heath, on one side by a small stream – once a lovely little river, full of fish, but now a dirty, stinking, polluted offence – and on the remaining sides by a railway goods-yard and housing estate respectively – the small farm gave some of the most wonderful and enjoyable pigeon shooting over decoys that one can imagine.

My friend, Ernie, had often told me about the sport he had enjoyed there. Sixty-odd pigeon one afternoon and then he ran out of cartridges: nearly a hundred birds on another, and so on. A short bus ride from his front door a 100-yard (91·45 m) walk, set up the decoys and within ten minutes start shooting! That was his invariable programme and I wonder how many shooters can enjoy such sport (for nothing, as he did) within the environs of such a large city. Moreover, Ernie, a true sportsman if ever there was one, a pretty shot, an expert alike with fly rod and with match equipment, generously shared his shooting facilities as often as he could with other, less fortunate, sportsmen.

When, therefore, Ernie phoned me and asked me if I would care to have an afternoon at the pigeons, I readily assented. From my North London home to Hounslow was not a long journey and as I set off, on that lovely August day, I hoped to be shooting within three-quarters of an hour. As I rode along on my faithful vintage motor-cycle I remembered the other days we had enjoyed together there, and, to add a little variation to the shooting I had, this time, brought a muzzle-loading single-barrel percussion 10-bore with me! From this I fired 1 oz. (28·3 g) of number 6 shot with 3 drams of black powder, the only wadding used being portions of daily paper, or pieces of toilet roll; the latter being better because the exact size and weight of the wad was automatically determined by the size of the paper, and there was thus no variation in the wadding. I have also found the tissue paper handkerchiefs excellent for this purpose.

However, shortly before I reached Hounslow itself, a terrific thunderstorm blew up and in the resultant downpour I was soaked to the skin. Before I could dismount from the machine and seek shelter I was drenched. There was only one thing to do, speed up and get through the rain as quickly as possible and hope to dry out on the shooting field.

When I arrived at Ernie's, we decided that the trip would be well worth making. The heavy rain, and hail, would have laid low some of the wheat and the pigeons would soon be on it. The peas would also provide a very fine temptation to the birds and, with the uncertainty of the weather, the usual stray pedestrians who, from time to time, wandered about over the shoot, would not put in an appearance.

The farm was made up of two or three large fields, each of which was divided from the other by a deep ditch, deep enough to stand in up to shoulder height. The ditches were plentifully covered by blackberry bushes and, of prime importance, were stone dry.

We chose for our shooting position a ditch between a field of barley and a field of peas. Part of the latter had been gathered and the wooden boxes to which I have earlier referred were lying about, ready to be built up into a hide into which Ernie presently disappeared. I took up my stand in a ditch, running parallel with and about twenty yards (18·3 m) from the goods-yard, and about 100 yards (91 m) from Ernie. With two dozen decoys out between us we were ready for the fun to begin.

Sure enough the birds came in and we started to shoot them. Watching the clock on the tower in the goods-yard I was able to time them: a bunch of birds every twelve to fifteen minutes, with odd birds between.

Now and again the skies clouded over and we had very heavy downpours of rain, which cause me considerable misgivings about the ignition system on my muzzle -loader.

But shots were plentiful, though there were disturbing incidents: when, for example, a local out for a stroll with his mongrel hound persisted, in spite of my frantic wavings, in walking into my area. To add insult to injury (he had no right to be there anyway) his dog made off with one of my decoys! The language which ensued equalled the thunder in its vehemence.

Then disaster overtook me. I had brought a cleaning rod with me to wipe out the barrel of my gun periodically. While watching Ernie bring off a terrific long shot at a low-flying bird, I managed, very carelessly, to break off the head of the rod in my tube! It was impossible to unscrew the breech-pin so I had to resort to manufacturing a hook from a safety-pin and thus to try to withdraw the broken part. At that moment Ernie joined me and together we worked on my gun. In the middle of our concentration a couple of woodies streaked past us. Ernie grabbed his gun, which was lying on my oilskin on the top of the ditch, swung up and fired twice, scoring one of the prettiest rights and lefts I have ever had the good fortune to witness – and at that same moment the obstruction cleared the muzzle of my gun.

Wet through, but happy, we completed the afternoon with two more birds each, then returned to Ernie's house where an excellent meal awaited us, followed by yarns of shooting and fishing until well into the night.

Unfortunately for Ernie, his shoot was gradually eaten away by building schemes. Now, where once he and his friends shot mallard and teal, scored feats amongst the partridges, bagged pheasant, and enjoyed first-rate pigeon decoying, there stands an ugly, red-rashed housing estate: the sign of 'progress' in a progressive world.

*February – Hertfordshire*

I left my basement flat about 7.30 in the morning and within half an hour was dropped by the London Transport omnibus outside the gate of the shoot. This shoot, somewhat similar to Ernie's, stands on the outskirts of London, with dormitory estates on three sides of it and the main A5 road to the North skirting the remaining boundary.

About 100 yards (91 m) back from this busy highway, there is a small copse, which formed part of the boundary of my shoot. This copse contains crab apple trees, oaks, firs, and elders. Insignificant, hardly to be noticed, it is the roost of several score of pigeons and a resort to which they make habitually throughout the day. In the early morning, by setting up decoys in a rough pasture, by the edge of a shallow pool, some quarter-mile from this wood, I hoped to attract birds whilst their crops were empty, when they were hungry and less wary. From near-by Hadley Woods I hoped that they would visit my pitch in scores throughout the early morning. And over the decoys, with my hide built into the shelter of a thick thorn hedge and shallow ditch, with a dead oak tree thirty yards (27·4 m) to my left, I hoped, using a ·410 firing the $2\frac{1}{2}$-inch (65 mm) case with 7 shot, to reduce their numbers a little.

The day was grey, and cold, with promise of rain. The wind blew in from the right direction, so that I was downwind of my decoys. For a full half-hour after I had placed my field nothing happened. I could see the flutter of wings in the top of the wood as pigeons moved from branch to branch. I was cold and feeling in my pocket for a cigarette when the first birds started to come in. My lofted decoy in the dead tree did its work well and a flock of fifteen birds settled in that tree. Carefully aiming the narrow tubes of my little double gun I took the *farthest* bird I had a clear view of and squeezed the trigger: I saw it hit and immediately turned my attention to the *nearest* bird which was clapping its wings in alarm as it left the tree. That didn't get far either. Two birds, one sitting and the other flying, wasn't a bad start to the day. I nipped out of my hide, collected the dead birds and set them up as decoys and returned to await developments.

For the next ninety minutes I had right royal sport. At the end of that time the flight slackened off and finally ceased. A quick check up showed that I had two cartridges left, so it was but the work of minutes to leave the field, catch a bus into the suburb, purchase a box of 'Fourlongs' and return to continue the sport.

I had intermittent shooting over the decoys for a further hour and then I decided to go into the copse. I placed the decoys in position about fifty yards (45·7 m) out from the wood and raised a lofted decoy into one of the oaks. A small clump of brambles made an excellent natural hide for me and I sat and waited for my pigeons which would, I well knew, come in.

The shooting that followed was slow. There were very long intervals between shots. When birds came, they flew in singly. But the little gun, with its slight report, and the fact that the birds were not in flocks, enabled me to choose fairly straightforward shots so that my average was pretty well four birds to five shots, which, for pigeon shooting, could be regarded as exceptionally good.

I left the shoot before dusk, leaving the birds to come in to roost in peace. I could hear other gunners blasting away over neighbouring farms and allotments, but I had taken a fair toll of my pigeons. Thirty-two birds in the bag was sufficient for me. As each bird weighs about 1¼ lb. (6·5 kg), it was a heavy enough load to carry even the short distance to my bus. Besides, I wanted to leave the roost undisturbed as I wanted to shoot there some other evening.

This may sound a contradiction to the real objects of pigeon shooting. In actual fact it was not. I was killing far more birds by the method I adopted than if I shot them at roost flight. Furthermore, I made certain that they would give me opportunity to make further inroads into their numbers. If I drove them away they might find other country where they could carry on practically unchecked.

*December – London Suburb*

The big gates were locked, the last of the visitors had left, and the large London cemetery was left to its silent occupants and the living who maintained it. From the foreman's house by the main gate two figures emerged into the gathering dusk. One, armed with a single-barrel ·410, made for a clump of oaks at the far end of the cemetery: the other, equipped with a single-barrel 12-bore, strode in the direction of the tall firs which overshadowed the new crematorium.

The cemetery was the roosting place of hundreds of pigeons which came in from the surrounding countryside and from the streets of London itself. The stock-doves and the domestic pigeons who had reverted to the wild state, rested on the roofs of the city's buildings, or under the eaves of bombed-out houses, but the wood-pigeons, greedy, careless because they feared no man in that huge sprawling mass called 'Town', flew in to the cemetery.

For ten minutes the flight lasted: for ten minutes the two gunners went to work. Birds were dropped, or missed, as they topped the crematorium: they were shot neatly by the ·410, used as a rifle, when they settled in the oaks, but all too soon the light faded and the sport was over.

Outside and around this queer sporting arena the familiar red double-deck buses rumbled, and the endless stream of London's rush hour crawled and stopped and crawled on again, lights appeared in windows, and the garish red and green neon lighting from a cinema became more and more dominant. This was, indeed, pigeon shooting in strange circumstances, but the two men concerned, working men and keen shots, had contrived to find some means of enjoying their sport which would otherwise have been denied them. The greatest care had, however, to be exercised in shooting. There was a vast danger area all round. The rattling of spent pellets on roofs, too much shooting, the dropping of dead or wounded birds beyond the cemetery wall, even the loss of dead birds in the cemetery itself, would have meant the withdrawal of the privilege, London citizens, dripping with sentimentality, would have objected in no uncertain manner had dead pigeons been picked up in the public highway. In consequence

Norman and Ted, the two men concerned, picked more or less certain shots, and I was always surprised to find how cleanly killed their birds were, and how few they ever lost.

*August – Middlesex*

The farm was moderately large – something over 300 acres (121·4 ha), and it had some fifty acres (20·2 ha) of woodland. The farmer, who had brought rough pastures under cultivation, re-drained and ditched the land, uprooted several small coppices and in the following year grown barley there, calculated that pigeons and rabbits reduced his profits by at least 15 to 20 per cent and in a bad year could turn his farming accounts into an actual loss. Like the Hertfordshire shoot, the farm was only thirty minutes by bus from Central London, yet when on the land it was possible to think oneself miles into the heart of the countryside.

The woods, extensive though they were, held very few pigeon at roost: they made their sanctuary in the woods of a large public park a mile or so away, where there was no great disturbance, except an annual drive by the rangers, and where visitors could be relied upon to leave remnants of picnic meals about. From these park sanctuaries the pigeons descended in huge flocks upon the peas and the corn my farmer sowed and *in one day* they cleared half an acre of newly sown wheat! I, along with two or three other gunners, keep up continual warfare against these birds, commencing in the February, and by mid-June, only odd pigeons were to be seen about the place. But, when the corn ripened, the pigeons returned, seemingly as numerous as ever.

One field, 'Forty Acre' the farmer called it, had suffered severe damage by gales and hailstorms and a considerable portion of the corn was beaten flat. Here the pigeons feasted, stealing the grain and fouling the corn with their droppings. The worst patch was some ten yards (9·1 m) or more in width, running for a length of sixty yards (54·8 m) into the field. At the deep ditch end of the field, where this patch ended, there was a tall oak and in this tree the pigeons perched, in scores, prior to dropping in to the beaten-down grain.

I chose a day when the wind blew directly from the beaten patch towards the oak tree and settled myself in the tall corn at the end of the beaten patch, so that I was well hidden. For good measure I added a few strands of grasses and corn to my hat, and was able to stand there, up to my eyes in the grain. I faced downwind to the oak tree and I had a clear view of the tree, the hinterland, and the corn-patch itself. The field rose steeply in a small hillock so that I was almost on a level with the top of the tree.

It was not necessary to set out decoys for this shooting as the pigeons would, I knew, come in to their feed in spite of any hard shooting which I might do. I had not long to wait before the first birds appeared. Their course was direct to the tree in front of me and they settled in, grunting to themselves, occasionally flapping a wing, and now and again moving from branch to branch. They appeared to be within arm's length of me, such was the optical illusion that the dip in the ground made, and had I not been experienced in wildfowling and pigeon shooting, I should in all probability have been tempted to stretch my gun and take a sitting shot at them.

I had two guns with me. One a double-barrel game gun, 12-bore, and the other a single-barrel muzzle-loading 10-bore from which I fired 1 oz. (28·3 g) of number 7 shot. Both guns were placed in front of me on two forked sticks, somewhat in the manner of an angler's rod rest, so that I should not tire myself by holding the weight of a gun for any length of time, yet both were handy to pick up and swing with the minimum of movement. Cartridges were ready to hand in a haversack to my left: the powder flask, shot pouch, wads, caps, and ramrod were placed conveniently to my right.

Presently a single bird flew down from the tree and dropped on to the beaten-down corn. He commenced to strut about, and finally to feed. I waited. I had plenty of time, and I wanted as many pigeon as possible on that patch in front of me. Within five minutes, at the most, I had twenty-two pigeons on that patch, feeding nearer and nearer to me. When the nearest bird was within fifteen yards (13·7 m) of me I gently reached for my double gun and took, with my choke barrel, a trio of birds feeding with heads together *on the ground.* At the report the blue cloud jumped with clapping wings, leaving their three comrades on the ground, dead. I swung on to one of the farthest birds and had the satisfaction of seeing him drop in a cloud of white feathers at the edge of the patch. Then, snatching up the muzzle-loader, I was still in time to swing on to the nearest bird, which by then was about thirty yards (27·4 m) away, and brought him down beautifully almost on top of the three killed by my sitting shot. Reloading the breech-loader I watched the startled birds swing round the patch in agitated flight and then come in to the killing area again.

Two more shots as the birds headed in, one bird down, and they were off, as fast as they could make it, in the direction of the park and safety. I went out to collect my bag and wondered how to term my first clash, five birds for three shots in the first instance – one a 'Right and left' and then the single. I resolved to call future shots of this description a 'Right, Left and Centre.'

By the time I had slipped two more cartridges into the game gun, re-loaded the muzzle-loader, capped it, and placed both guns in the forked sticks, the pigeons were already heading back for the oak tree.

For the space of an hour and a half I shot those birds until both they, and I, had had enough. At the end of this time I had exhausted a box of cartridges, half a flask of powder and 2 lb. (0·9 kg) of shot. Fifty-seven shots fired and forty-three pigeons collected.

The idea of the ground shot at the three birds may not seem 'sporting' to the average shooting man. My obligation to the farmer was to *kill* as many pigeons as possible: to this end I fired half a dozen shots at birds on the ground and collected eleven pigeons that way. The rest of the shooting was sporting shooting, and some tricky shots were presented, I may add. Thus, in the one operation, I had excellent sport and at the same time I did my farmer host a good turn.

The muzzle-loading gun, with its open boring and light shot load, might appear to the uninitiated to have been the best gun to bring into action in the first place, using the modern game gun, with its more constricted muzzles and longer range afterwards. My reason for using the game-gun first was that I was taking the longer shots and following it up with the more open spread of the shot from the muzzle-loader. Furthermore, black powder when fired from a gun, unless there is a very high wind, obstructs the view of the sportsman and often prevents him from seeing whether a bird has been hit or not, and if hit sometimes prevents his marking its fall. The 'smoke of battle' was a very real thing in black-powder days. To have fired my muzzle-loader first would have been to unduly handicap myself. Always, when shooting at pigeon near at hand take the farthest birds first, you then have a second chance at the nearer ones.

I kept up this kind of campaign for several days, with varying success. The essential factor for success was that the wind should blow from me to the birds – a reversal of the usual procedure when decoying as, had I been using decoys, they would have been down-wind of me.

*May – Midlothian*

This was a rather unusual expedition after pigeons. The scene was a field of newly mown hay and the pigeons literally made the ground blue with their packed bodies as they fed on the grass seeds. Shooting from hides of built up hay-cocks, my friend Hamish and I came to moderate terms with these birds, but only in the first hour or two after dawn. During the remainder of the day they came in only as single birds and decoying was not very successful – probably because there was such good feeding ground in the vicinity where they were not harassed.

'My goodness,' exclaimed Hamish, when we arrived on the scene early one morning, and saw the vast flocks of pigeons occupying the field. 'If only we could punt to them.' At first I thought he had gone out of his mind: I knew that Hamish had done a little fowling at nearby Gullane and Aberlady, but, to the best of my knowledge he had never punted to wildfowl, and the idea of his punting to pigeons over dry land convinced me that he had gone soft in the head.

I determined to humour him.

'Okay,' I agreed. 'But what about the gun?'

'The very thing——' he remarked, looking at the pigeons, 'The very thing——' He kept saying the same thing over and over again and I resolved to bring him back to his senses. 'For heaven's sake man,' I said, 'forget it. You must realize there's no ditch here you can bring a canoe up, you couldn't even float a life-belt up the small dyke at the back of the farm, and as for shooting them with a puntgun.'

'I'll do it,' he said. And beyond that he refused to say anything. Properly nettled by his behaviour, I failed miserably at the pigeons that morning, while Hamish, engrossed in his ideas of punting to them, failed to hit a single bird.

It was later that same evening that he unfolded his plan to me, as he showed me his 'punt' in the tool-shed at the side of his house.

A few seasons earlier he had been present when a rusty weapon was unearthed from the accumulated debris and junk of years in the attic of a public house which was changing hands. The then licensee of the public house had not known of this gun before and was as surprised as everyone else at its discovery. It was a percussion cap muzzle-loader, with a barrel length of 60 inches (1·52 m), and it weighed just 28 lb. (12·7 kg). The stock was of conventional pattern, though with a rather large bend and terminated in a solid brass butt-plate. The trigger guard was as broad as the hilt of a claymore.

The muzzle diameter was just over 1⅛ inches (28·5 mm) and though it had every appearance of a shoulder gun, its weight and enormous barrel length made it appear that at some time it must have been fired from a rest. It could hardly have been designed for sporting purposes. As for a puntgun, the conventional stock militated against that idea.

No one present had wanted the gun and my friend Hamish very proudly took possession of it. Spiders were dislodged from the barrel when cleaning began, but by good soakings in paraffin and with plenty of elbow grease, he did make it presentable and got it into decent enough condition to hang over his fireplace.

Of course, being a true gun fan, the day came when he *had* to test it. Fearful of bursting the barrel, he tested 'Old Alice', as he called the gun, with a standard 12-bore load, and the result was disappointing in its pop-gun like effect. The gun was cleaned and replaced over the fireplace where it remained until I saw it in the tool-shed that evening.

He then, grandly, announced his plan. Under the influence of Col. Peter Hawker (who would probably have turned in his grave had he learned of Hamish's intentions) whose works he had read, and of which I was ignorant at that time, he had constructed what he called his 'land carriage'. What in actual fact he had constructed was a contraption rather like a large T-square, mounted on two old perambulator wheels. His idea was to lash the old gun on to it, push it up to the feeding pigeons, and then wham!

He decided, by what calculation I do not know (and knowing the implications now I shudder!) that a suitable load would be 8 oz. (226·4 g) of No. 4 shot propelled by no less than 20 drams of black powder! I was against this experiment on account of the age and unknown condition of the gun. There was plenty of metal in the barrels, which had sometime previously been shortened to their 60 inches (1·5 m), and the breech looked strong, but! . . .

However, I assisted him to load the T-square, and the gun, into the car and arranged to visit the farm with him the following morning.

We got to the field in good time and behind cover of a thick thorn hedge, in a sunken lane, Hamish lashed the gun to its 'carriage' with stout rope, then loaded her, ramming the charge home with a brush steel. He tied a piece of cord to the trigger and passed it through a screw-eye on the carriage. This was to act as a lanyard.

Finally, he decked out the whole contraption with bunches of hay, twigs, etc., and wheeled it through the gate leading into the field. Presently the first pigeons began to come in, followed by larger flocks, and in a half hour the field was covered with large blue patches of feeding birds. The big moment had arrived!

Hamish lay down beside the gun, then pushing with his legs in the manner of a swimmer doing the breast-stroke, but with frequent pauses, he kicked that artillery piece out towards the nearest flock of birds. In spite of his earnest invitations to join him I refused to go, pointing out (though it did not deceive him) that I would only be in his way and might spoil his sport. After he set out on his journey I took myself a safe distance away, far enough to be safe from flying portions of burst barrel, and watched the proceedings.

About sixty yards (58·8 m) from the nearest group of birds he brought his cannon to rest. Suddenly, with a colossal roar and amid a great cloud of white smoke, he opened fire. Pieces of flying paper drifted about in the air. In the near-by farmyard a dog commenced to yap hysterically, and a couple of fields away I saw a stallion running about in wild circles, kicking his legs in the air. The astounded pigeon took off with a clatter and disappeared immediately – *and not a single bird remained dead on the ground, or dropped in flight.*

For a few moments a cloud of smoke obscured Hamish and his secret weapon, and as it began to clear I heard groans and anguished cries coming from him. Fearing the worst, I ran over to him, and although he was a sorry sight, with a cut head, two beautiful shiners, and a tooth missing from his dentures, he was otherwise unhurt. The barrel had not burst. But overlooking the fact that the gun had been lashed to the carriage when he lay beside it, he had not reckoned on the effect of recoil. The whole thing had jumped up and back with the discharge and he had been belted beautifully by the T-piece. Additionally he stank to high heaven of powder. And no pigeon! Hamish didn't try the experiment again, and thus ended the magnificent failure.

If clearing the ground of pigeon was the idea, then that also was a failure, for in spite of their alarm and the terrific blast from the gun, the pigeons were back again as normal the following day.

*November – Essex*

I received the invitation to a roost shoot just as I was contemplating a trip to the Blackwater after the widgeon. For once I decided to forego the fowling and take my chance amongst the woodies. Good sport was promised and with the inducement of half-price cartridges, I found myself at the rendezvous before the appointed hour.

The plan was simplicity itself. The pigeons roosted in a large wood which formed the northern boundary of the estate. But there were two smaller coppices into which the birds might fly. There were ten guns, one of whom I had met before, and we were asked to take up positions forty yards (36·5 m) apart, along the face of the wood. It was suggested that one or two of us might like to stand in the vicinity of the little coppices, but that was optional.

We took up position at 3.30 and I was surprised to find that most of my companions stood on the outside of the wood, under the branches of the trees, gazing upwards into the sky looking for pigeons. However, I bided my time and though I was doubtful if there would be much success attendant on this venture, I watched and waited.

About 3.45 the pigeon started to come in. Firstly as single birds, then in larger bodies, finally in huge flocks. At one period there was a never-ending line of them and I counted 110 birds before giving up the task. My worst fears were realized. My left-hand companion, wearing a natty suit of plus-fours, carrying a 20-bore, and a green Tyrolean hat with a mallard feather in it, proceeded to open fire on every bird which came within 100 yards (91 m) of him. My next-but-one neighbour stepped out into the field some fifty yards (45 m) from the wood and proceeded to shoot all round 360 degrees! At this point I went to the organizer and told him I proposed to shoot the coppices. I think he saw through me, but only smiled and agreed.

I took up my stand behind the coppice, so that any birds coming in would top the trees in front of me, and just be in range long enough for me to connect. But owing to the heavy barrage going on behind me, what birds there were came in very high indeed. I need hardly add that something like 200 shots were fired by the gunners behind me, and that although several 'hard hit' birds were claimed – only one bird was produced for the bag. 'Terrific sport,' crowed Plus-Fours, 'Fired two boxes off, terrific.'

His cartridges were not half-price – but I did wonder at the cost to the community of the other 12-bore users, wasting subsidized cartridges to that extent. As a pigeon *shoot*, it was useless, an utter failure, but, at least, it was an experience.

Nevertheless, invited to the same shoot on another occasion, with a good pigeon shot as organizer, and a few words by myself on the art of concealment and silence, the bag was an average of five birds per gun, i.e. fifty birds in all, though less pigeons flew in. In this case I doubt if more than seventy shots were fired altogether. The trouble is that when some idiot fires at high or impossible birds, within a short time less experienced sportsmen follow suit, and the shooting deteriorates. A successful battue is one in which sportsmen concerned exercise restraint in the use of the trigger finger. A good pigeon drive is not measured by shots fired, but by the way in which those shots are fired. A battue at which fifty guns are present and only twenty-five shots fired, accounting for twenty birds is a better pigeon battue than one where ten guns fire 200 shots and bring down forty birds.

Of course I have enjoyed other pigeon-shooting days: there were often occasions when I performed badly, fortunately, without other gunners to witness my bungling efforts in throwing charge after charge of shot into the air recently vacated by the birds. There were occasions, too, when things went right, when the birds came in and my aim was true, days when I could not miss. But every day was a day enjoyed. And I can honestly say that I have often enjoyed a day when I have bagged but a single bird equally as well as a day when my bag has been as much as I could carry.

Pigeons are rightly termed the most difficult of all sporting birds. It is only right that they should be placed, irrespective of their label of vermin, at the top of the list of the shooter's quarry. Noble they may not be, though *worthy* they undoubtedly are.

CHAPTER 11

# *Pigeon Pie*

From Roman times pigeons have been valued as a delicacy, and today, with less meat available the pigeon is likely to come into its own again as a useful food.

Pigeons, in spite of the old fallacy about their liability to kill the person who feeds off them too often, are a good, rich food. They may be eaten all the year round, and can be served up in a variety of ways: stewed, casseroled, fried, roasted, boiled, and in pies.

Throughout the country there may be seen pigeon cotes where these birds were reared expressly for table purposes. But not every person was entitled to keep pigeons, and the ownership of a *columbarium* (or pigeon cote) depended upon certain social or landed qualifications – for example, the lordship of the manor. In addition to these restrictions on columbarium ownership, pigeons were protected by very severe laws. In the sixteenth century a third conviction for pigeon house-breaking could be punished by death. By an Act of James I, the shooting of house-doves or pigeons or the taking or destroying of them by nets, or any instruments or engines whatever, rendered the offender liable to a term of imprisonment for three months or a fine of 20s. (no mean sum in those days) for every bird and he became bound by recognizances not to shoot at, kill, take, or destroy any of the birds, including pigeons and house-doves, mentioned in the Act.

By the same Act (1 Jac. I., c. 27) every person keeping hawks and licensed to shoot 'hail-shot in hand-guns or birding pieces' at crow, chough, pie, rook, *ring-dove*, jay, or smaller birds for hawk's meat only, might shoot and kill hawk's meat according to the licence, but such person was not to shoot within 100 paces of any pigeon-house.

For shooting at pigeons with intent to kill, the statute 2 Geo. II, enacted that the penalty be 20s., viz: the same as for killing one bird under James I's Act. It was further laid down that for prosecutions under George II's legislation, information for proceedings must be laid within two months.

The pigeon-house served two purposes. Firstly it housed the birds, secondly the birds' droppings were collected from the floor of the house for the sake of the very valuable manure. It is believed that the ancient Persians were the originators of this practice, though this belief cannot be substantiated. Certainly, too, the ancient Israelites knew the value of pigeons both as a food and as a sacrificial bird in their various ceremonies, and Talmudical enactments were made, giving protection to dove-houses and their occupants, and even the siting of these buildings was carefully regulated.

The Roman Empire was one of the most extravagant that ever existed: certainly the chief Roman citizens explored every appetizing delicacy. Pigeons figured in many Roman menus and Varro records (*circa* 36 B.C.) that the name of *Columbae* was given to pigeons on account of the Roman habit of building pigeon-houses on the gable-ends, or *columen*, of the farmstead. So highly were pigeons rated that the Romans hired men specially, so Columella records, to chew up the bread used for pigeon feeding.

During late years, however, the pigeon has fallen from his high place. The provision of cheap food in great abundance before the late war ousted him from the family menu, and only with the rationing of food during the war and for a short time afterwards, did the pigeon regain any popularity as a table bird. Today he provides a cheap, tasty, nourishing dish though from the professional pigeon shooter's point of view, his price is far too low. The pigeon shooter, however, has the great advantage that he knows the condition of the birds, and (if we are to believe opinions expressed by some psychologists) by eating the bird he has shot the hunter atones for his guilt! Certainly the eating of pigeon shot by oneself, is a very pleasant way of 'atoning for guilt'.

Pigeons are not everyman's dish. To some people they are delightful, while others have a distinct aversion to them. Generally the most popular way of serving pigeons is in the traditional English pie. But this needs a considerable addition of beef steak and hard-boiled eggs to give it bulk, while strong stock is necessary to give body and 'set' if the pie is to be consumed cold. There are other, more exciting methods to use, and in the following notes I shall refer only to pigeons and not to 'squabs', delicious though they are.

*Casserole of pigeons' breasts.* Do not utilize the whole bird. Cut off the breasts, neglecting the back and legs. With the addition of lightly fried carrots, onions, and half a dozen stoned olives, such a casserole is a very good dish. The whole should be served with peas, and other vegetables to choice.

*Stuffed pigeon.* Pluck and draw the bird. Wash it inside and clean well. Mince the heart with an equal quantity of mushrooms and bind the stuffing with the yolk of an egg. Add pepper and salt. Sew up the bird to secure the stuffing and then cover the breast of the bird with a rasher of fat bacon. Roast in a very hot oven.

*Italian pigeons.* This is a very attractive Continental way of cooking the birds by the 'sweet-sour' method. Pluck, draw, and joint the bird then cook it very slowly (say two hours) in a cupful of wine vinegar to which has been added two chopped onions, three tablespoons of tomato juice, a little chopped celery. Add a few stoned olives and a little salt. Sugar should be added to taste, and, need one add, a little garlic to complete the dish.

*Casserole pigeon.* Skin or pluck the birds and clean them, washing them out with salty water. Place the birds in a casserole to which has been added half an onion, a little mace, salt and pepper. Cover with water. Place in a slow oven (the best method is to allow overnight cooking on the lowest control) and the birds, no matter what their age, will be found to be tender. Serve with chipped or roast potatoes and green peas. This is a very simple, popular method of cooking.

*Roast pigeons.* Pluck, draw, and clean. Stuff the birds with forcemeat, to which 'Panade' has been added. This is simply the white crust of bread which has been thoroughly soaked in milk and put into a saucepan with a little butter. This is then strained and amalgamated over low heat until smooth. Mixed with the forcemeat it makes it very much lighter. Place the birds in a roasting tin with a little bacon over the breast and allow 20–30 minutes for cooking time.

*Fried pigeons.* Quarter the birds. Wash the quarters in salt water and add a little pepper. Fry them in hot fat until dark golden brown on both sides and serve hot on toast or with chipped potatoes.

Alternatively, dip the quarters in batter and fry as cutlets.

*Pigeon Pâté.* Quarter the birds. Bone the legs. Lightly fry the quarters and then bed them in a pie dish lined with bacon. Interlay the birds with pork forcemeat. Moisten well with a good stock adding herbs or seasoning to taste. Cover with a paste crust and then cook in the usual way. If desired chestnuts or button mushrooms, or eggs (hard boiled), may be added to this very delightful pie.

*Braised Pigeon with Olives.* Pluck and draw the pigeons (two for four people) and remove the legs and breasts in sides of one piece. Then make a stock from the remainder of the carcass and giblets (but not the livers). To make this stock, place the carcasses and giblets in about half a pint of water, add one or two carrots and half an onion. Allow two hours for cooking in an ordinary pan, though a pressure cooker should reduce this time to half an hour. Other ingredients required are: 2 oz. (56·7 g) of fat, 4 rashers of bacon, 2 dessertspoons of flour, a dozen stoned olives, ½ teaspoonful mixed herbs, a large onion, ½ lb. of carrots.

Melt the fat into a casserole and fry up the bacon, which should have been chopped into small pieces. Add chopped-up onion and carrots and fry until brown, then add the herbs and slowly stir in the flour. Gradually work in the half-pint of stock and stir it well. Finally add the olives and pieces of pigeon and cook them in a low oven for at *least* two hours.

To serve – fry some rounds of thick bread (or make a similar quantity of toast) lay a pigeon leg and breast on each, arrange the olives and pour the hot sauce over the lot.

*Sauces.* It is an axiom that only good cooks know good sauces. It is a further axiom that good sauces make the dish. The two following recipes are ideal sauces for serving with pigeons.

*Mushroom Sauce.* Ingredients 8 oz. (227 g) of button mushrooms, 1 oz. (28·3 g) of butter or margarine, 1 teaspoonful lemon juice, 1 dessertspoonful cornflour, half a pint of brown stock, 2 tablespoonfuls of cream or tinned milk.

Peel and stalk the mushrooms and cut them into quarters. Put them in a small saucepan and add the butter and lemon juice and cook slowly for about ten minutes. Add the half-pint of brown stock: simmer for half an hour. Mix the cornflour with the cream, add this to the mushrooms and stir in well. Cook a further few minutes then serve. This, incidentally, makes an excellent sauce for the stuffed-pigeon recipe.

*Vinegar Sauce.* This is sometimes termed Sauce Piquante and can be added to any pigeon dish, particularly casserole or roast pigeons.

Ingredients: half a gill (71 ml) of malt vinegar, 1 tablespoonful chopped capers, a small gherkin, ½ oz. (14·2 g) butter, small onion, ½ oz. (14·2 g) flour, half a pint (284 ml) brown stock, some chopped parsley.

Put the vinegar, chopped capers and the gherkin (also chopped into small pieces) into a saucepan and simmer until the vinegar has been reduced to half. Then melt the butter in a saucepan, allow it to brown, then add the small onion (cut into slices), and stir until that is browned also. Add the flour, stirring in well, add the brown stock and bring to the boil. Allow to simmer for a further twenty minutes, then strain. Add to the vinegar, bring to the boil, and add the parsley immediately prior to serving.

None of the foregoing require the skill of a qualified chef. All the ingredients are obtainable readily in any grocery shop.

With a little ingenuity, the addition of Madeira or Port, redcurrant jelly, or (good old Scottish recipe) the addition of rowan jelly, the amateur cook can ring the changes as often as he (or she) likes and, in his (or her) own kitchen prepare from the humble pigeon a dish comparable with any which might be served in the most exclusive West End hotel.

A little imagination in the manner in which the cooked bird is presented, as for example, on a bed of cooked rice, on fried bread garnished with asparagus, cold in aspic with salad, in addition to the conventional roast and baked or chipped potatoes and peas, should go a long way to dispelling that unfortunately popular notion that pigeons are monotonous on the table, and indigestible to boot.

Finally, when dressing birds for the table the shooter, if he does this job himself (which he should), would be advised to carry out post-mortem examinations of the birds. The crops should be examined and their contents noted, and counted if possible, the result of this examination being entered into the pigeon-shooting diary to which I have referred previously. Then the plucked or skinned carcass should be examined for traces of pellets. Sometimes the sportsman may be astonished to find that out of his total charge of shot, the bird has been killed by a solitary pellet in the head, or heart. It goes without saying that unusually large specimens should be weighed both with and without the crop. The plumage should also be looked at to see whether or not there are interesting variations. Finally, look for rings, though only a few birds have been ringed for recording purposes, it may well be that one such bird falls into the shooter's possession. The ring should be returned to the appropriate authority whose name it bears, together with a brief note as to where it met its end and when, and its condition when shot. In addition to an acknowledgement the shooter will be informed, as matter of interest, when and where the bird was ringed.

Any unusually marked or deformed specimen should be sent to the local museum for examination. In this manner the sportsman can contribute towards the increase of knowledge concerning these birds, about which we still know very little.

For its gentle song in the spring, typical of the English countryside; for its fast, tricky, wariness in flight, which tests his marksmanship and the craftsmanship of the gunsmith; for days spent in the countryside; for, perhaps, his only opportunity of sporting shooting; and finally, for its culinary properties, the average shooting man owes a great debt to the pigeon.

In the previous pages I have endeavoured to introduce the novice to the pleasures of pigeon shooting: and I can close on no better note than the excellent advice given by George Markland in *Pteryplegia, or, The Art of Shooting Flying*, wherein he says:

'I am sensible there is no becoming *Sportsmen* by Book. You may here find the *Rules* and proper Directions for that End; but practice alone can make you *Masters*.'

# Index